For Joel and Claire, who always glitter

Panning *for* Gold *in the* Kitchen Sink

Everyday Creative Writing

Michael C. Smith
Suzanne Greenberg

NTC Publishing Group

Library of Congress Cataloging-in-Publication Data

Smith, Michael C. (Michael Cecil)
    Panning for gold in the kitchen sink : everyday creative writing / Michael C.
  Smith, Suzanne Greenberg.
        p.   cm.
    Includes bibliographical references and indexes.
    ISBN 0-658-00228-7
    1. Authorship.   2. Creative writing.   I. Greenberg, Suzanne.   II. Title.
  PN153.S65   2000
  808'.02—dc21   99-33424
                                                                                                          CIP

Cover design by Amy Yu Ng
Interior design by Nicole Bender

Published by NTC Publishing Group
A division of NTC/Contemporary Publishing Group, Inc.
4255 West Touhy Avenue, Lincolnwood (Chicago), Illinois 60646-1975 U.S.A.
Printed in the United States of America
International Standard Book Number: 0-658-00228-7
99 00 01 02 03 04 MV 19 18 17 16 15 14 13 12 11 10 9 8 7 6 5 4 3 2 1

Contents

Down the Street 77

In the Gold Mine 125

Assaying: How Do You Know It's Gold? 175

From Nuggets to Artifacts:
Finishing What You Started 187

Gold Futures: Prospects for Publication 199

Preface

Have you ever seen a movie or read a biography about a writer's wildly adventurous and unconventional life and sighed in weary envy as the credits rolled or you turned the last page? Maybe you went away hopeful and even inspired about writing yourself, and it wasn't until the next day that the predictability of your own life hit you. Perhaps it happened while you were taking the same route to work that you take every morning or doing the coupon math in the supermarket after work or washing dishes while your kids fought over who guessed the phrase first on "Wheel of Fortune."

The truth is that this is the kind of life that most of us live, writers included. Sure, there are exceptions. A few writers have grants that fund their writing and allow them to pursue their craft in a leisurely fashion while looking out a window in an Italian villa. But only a small number of writers make enough money by writing to work full-time at it. Most are forced by the necessities of economics to have a "real" job, too, or, by the necessity of their circumstances, to raise children or care for older relatives. The book you are holding presumes that the life you are living now is already the writer's life. We believe that inspiring ideas can be found in the everyday, even in the murky soap bubbles in the kitchen sink, and the exercises in this book are designed to lead you to those ideas.

The book gets the "panning for gold" part of its title from one of possibly an infinite number of metaphors for the writer: that of being a prospector, a forty-niner, who continues the search for gold long after the main veins have been tapped and after everyone has given up. What this prospector discovers is that the plain rocks and jackrabbit bones usually discarded have their own luster and that virtually anything that we encounter can be valuable once touched with our efforts and marked with our individual signature.

Creative writing is too often seen as the exclusive preserve of university writing programs, and there's no denying that extensive reading and institutions of higher learning can provide the material and context in which creative writing can be understood in a fuller historical and critical way. But whether or not they are affiliated with writing programs, many people still play with words, spin yarns, write amusing anecdotes. People who write creatively do so for the same reasons that others sing or dance or play instruments or paint: to express something of their true selves; to reflect on what they did, thought, or felt; to capture evanescent truths or produce moments of beauty—and sometimes just to let others know that they were here.

Modern psychology and self-help movements perhaps exaggerate the importance of our knowing ourselves, but we believe that in the world of creative writing, it is not an exaggeration to say that the genuine is the individual. Provide others with your unique take on the world, your own angle, your imaginative fingerprint or DNA code, and you have provided a gift more valuable than gold. The exercises in this book are designed to help you extract that gift. They give you hundreds of sites in which to dig for your life and recover previous ore.

This is a book of writing exercises for students, teachers, and writers, whether they are professional or amateur, beginning or advanced, committed or dabbling; anyone who wants to write something creative but can't quite get started, has temporary writer's block, or simply enjoys a new challenge will enjoy this book. It is a book for those who sometimes prefer to do rather than to think and read about doing. We believe that what distinguishes writers from other sorts of people is that, first and foremost, writers write. If you complete these exercises, regardless of how you complete them and regardless of the quality or merits of the results, you will be doing what creative writers do.

ACKNOWLEDGMENTS

We received much support from colleagues and friends as we worked on the first and second editions of this book. We wish, first, to thank our reviewers of the original text—Allen Woodman, Northern Arizona University; Art Homer, the Writer's Workshop, University of Nebraska at Omaha; and Patricia Bridges, Norfolk State University—who offered us excellent advice as we worked toward our final draft, and, second, the reviewers whose valuable suggestions guided us as we grappled with what to change and what to leave alone in this second edition: Anne Calcagno, DePaul University; Scott M. Fisher, Rock Valley College; and Bonnie Flaig, Kalamazoo Valley Community College.

Special thanks to all our friends and family who put up with us as we wrote—and then rewrote—this book. In particular, we would like to thank Gina Sawin, who patiently listened to us talk our way through the book before it was a book; Joyce and Gary Lott, who offered us their support and expertise on the first edition; and Larry Greenberg, Gina Caruso, and Sarah Michaelson, who have for as long as we can remember unfailingly believed in the strength of our ideas and words.

The second edition of this book finds us living in a new location with new teaching positions and friends and, therefore, a whole host of new folks to thank. The faculty of the English Department at California State University, Long Beach, where Suzanne teaches creative writing, have been especially notable in their support of this project. Department Chair Eileen Klink deserves special acknowledgment for her constant encouragement, as does College of Liberal Arts dean Dorothy Abrahamse. In addition, Suzanne would like to thank the creative writing faculty at CSULB for their support. And at UCLA, where Michael teaches in the Writing Programs, we would like to thank Cheryl Giuliano and Bruce Beiderwell for their support and encouragement.

Friends and family members who endured far too many updates about how the second edition was going have earned our complete gratitude for their patience with us. In particular, we'd like to thank Cornel Bonca and Teddi Chichester Bonca, role models for us in their ability to finish serious work with young children underfoot. In addition, we'd like to thank Jan Kraft, Ana Kothe, Jennifer Woods, Ginger Mazzapica, Beth Lau, Elizabeth Young, Mimi Hotchkiss, Tamarah Hardesty, Anne and Jim Poppaw, Angelin and Dave Tubman, Madelyn and Michael Callahan, Emily and Steve Piro, all great friends and experts at life balancing acts themselves. Family members who helped us become who we are and who we still might be all deserve thanks for their influence: Sean Carter, Morton and Barbara Ann Greenberg, Kim Greenberg, Elizabeth Greenberg and Robert Blecker and Florence and David Feinstein.

A very special thanks to Ada Ramirez, who consistently provided our children with loving attention when our attention was turned, by necessity, elsewhere.

We are supremely indebted to our original editor, Marisa L. L'Heureux, who promised she would work with us from start to finish and kept her word. We quickly came to count on her gentle, reasonable counsel and astute observations at important stages in our writing and editing processes, as well as her sense of perspective and humor.

In addition, we wish to thank the editor of this second edition, Andy Winston, whose expertise on an infinite number of areas was, perhaps, overshadowed only by his ability to put up with us as we struggled mightily to meet his very reasonable deadlines. It was a great pleasure working with Andy on this second edition.

Finally, we wish to thank our students at California State University, Long Beach; UCLA Writing Programs; Howard University; the University of Maryland; Bowie State University; and the Maryland-National Park and Planning Commission, whose creative energies demanded so much new material from us each week that they left us no choice but to finally write a book.

Introduction

This collection of creative writing invention exercises is organized into seven sections—**Provisions and Prospecting Tools, Around the House, Down the Street, In the Gold Mine, Assaying: How Do You Know It's Gold?, From Nuggets to Artifacts: Finishing What You Started,** and **Gold Futures: Prospects for Publication**.

The first section, **Provisions and Prospecting Tools,** outfits you with both basic and less common writing equipment: freewriting, brainstorming, free association, listing, and computer gaming, among others. We also include in this section a discussion of how to determine what form—for example, poetry, fiction, or creative nonfiction—your exercise might best be cast in. You may choose to read **Provisions and Prospecting Tools** first, or you may want to dig right into the three middle sections that are the core of the book.

The **Around the House** section includes exercises that use as creative writing resources things, processes, and behaviors with which you are intimately familiar, including your family, chores, and routines. The **Down the Street** section exploits your experiences with the outside world, including work, travel, and romance. **In the Gold Mine** gathers creative writing exercises that make use of abstract ideas, fantasies, dreams, emotions, lies, promises, play, and pure speculation. All of these exercises work equally well with poetry, fiction, or creative nonfiction (we use the terms *creative nonfiction* and *essay* interchangeably to mean prose writing that is significantly fact-based).

The fifth section of the book, **Assaying: How Do You Know It's Gold?** provides suggestions for how to evaluate what you've found in your digging in order to help you identify the work that might merit further development and refinement.

The sixth section, **From Nuggets to Artifacts: Finishing What You Started,** offers tips on how to continue if you find yourself stuck, as, inevitably, we all do from time to time in writing a story, poem, or essay.

The final section, **Gold Futures: Prospects for Publication,** provides guidelines for submitting your finished work for possible publication.

Each exercise in the middle three sections contains background and instructions for getting started on two different levels: what we call "Panning Instructions" and "Excavating Instructions." In many cases, but not in all, the "Excavating Instructions" ask you to go "deeper" into your material. For example, in the exercise entitled "Getting Lost and Finding the Way," the "Panning Instructions" relate to getting actually and geographically lost, while the "Excavating Instructions" ask you to explore situations in which you couldn't find your way emotionally, logically, or spiritually. In some cases, the two sets of instructions simply address different angles of the same subject. Read over both sets of instructions before you begin, and choose the set that inspires you the most at the moment.

We give examples of actual outcomes—what we call "Nuggets"—for each exercise and examples of published work—what we call "Artifacts"—that relate in some way to the exercises. Some of our exercises grew out of these published pieces; sometimes the published works were incorporated because they illustrate some aspect of the exercise or relate generally to the exercise's subject.

The exercises ask you to explore a variety of topics drawn largely from everyday life, and in most cases the exercises suggest specific approaches to the topics. However, you will undoubtedly veer away from the topics and approaches suggested to pursue your own ideas and inclinations. Ultimately, there may be very little similarity between what the exercise instructions ask for and what you write, and that's fine. To derive the greatest benefit from this book, remain open to all the possibilities generated and suggested by your own imagination as you do the exercises, even if this takes you away from the approach suggested for the exercise. It will help to maintain a sense of serious playfulness throughout your writing. In other words, adopt an attitude not so oppressively serious that your responses get predictable, nor so wildly fun-loving that only silliness is possible. While we have tried to provide detailed instructions for the completion of each exercise, as long as you are writing something, there is no "correct" or "incorrect." The book's primary objective, and our greatest hope, is that in doing the exercises you will get caught up in the interplay between your imagination and the act of writing.

Regardless of your ultimate writing goals—publication, self-expression, and so forth—we recommend that you use this book as a way of jumping directly into writing when you don't have any particular form (story, poem, essay) or subject in mind. All you need to know is that you want to write something of a creative nature. If you're not familiar with the prewriting tools we describe in the **Provisions and Prospecting Tools** section, such as freewriting, brainstorming, listing, and clustering, you might want to familiarize yourself with these before you try a writing exercise. Alternatively, you can simply choose any exercise in any of the three exercise sections and get started on it. Then, if a writing tool with which you are not familiar is mentioned (the terms for these are printed in bold), turn back to **Provisions and Prospecting Tools** and learn about the tool and how to use it.

We believe that the act of writing itself ultimately will suggest the form to which your beginning efforts should lead. If you are not particularly familiar with poetry, fiction, or creative nonfiction, however, the last part of the **Provisions and Prospecting Tools** section—"What Form Should You Choose?"—can help you in deciding whether you should work on a story, a poem, or a piece of creative nonfiction.

We would love you to read this book from cover to cover and complete each exercise in the order presented, though we recognize that doing so would result in your writing an incredible amount of material. You may be using the book in a creative writing class in which specific exercises are assigned and discussed on a schedule, or you might use it as a source of group challenges in one of the thousands of writing groups that have sprung up over the last few years. You may be a lone writer using it in search of just a few notions to get you started; you might, from time to time, skim the text and light on an exercise or an aspect of an exercise that inspires you. Indeed, there is no right or wrong way of using this book, so long as the result is writing.

What this book does not do, however, is offer specific instruction in the techniques of writing poetry, fiction, or creative nonfiction. There are a lot of books already that do this very well, and for those who are interested in this kind of guidance, we recommend some specific texts in the **For Further Reading** section at the end of the book. In addition, many writers learn technique through reading, and we hope that some of these exercises inspire you not only to write, but to search out more work by the published writers to whom we introduce you in each section.

Where you go from here is up to you. Gold can be cast into many forms: delicate chains, durable wedding bands, and even magical chalices. Some of these exercises may yield nuggets beautiful in their own right, while others may benefit from further shaping and forming. Wherever these exercises lead you, we hope you enjoy the prospecting.

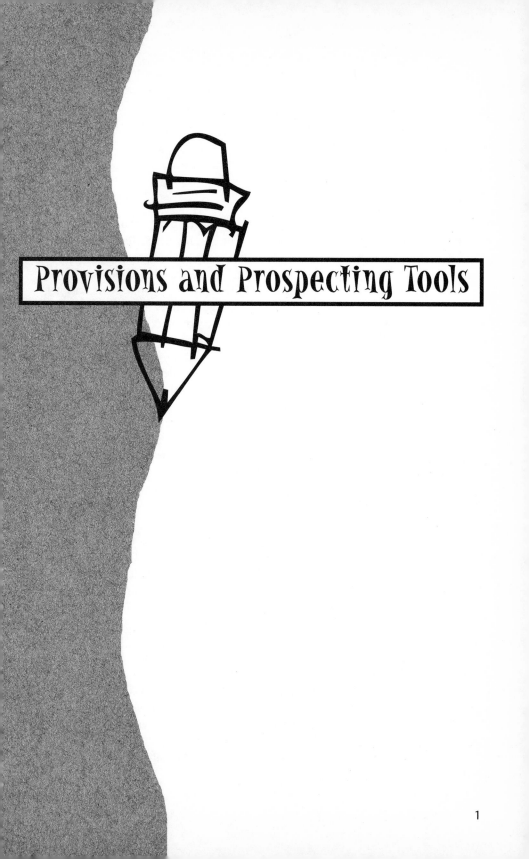

Provisions and Prospecting Tools

You might think that all a writer really needs to get started are a few blank sheets of paper and a couple of durable pens. Technically, you would be right. While a scuba diver, skier, or bungee jumper has to buy or rent elaborate, expensive equipment, many excellent poems, stories, novels, and essays have been written longhand by people with meager incomes and serious misgivings about technology. Writers need rich imaginations more than they need padded bank accounts or elaborate machines. Of course, having use of a computer or word processor is a bonus (more on that later), but many of the provisions and tools you will need most as you begin on your journey are far less tangible than a color monitor or a hard drive.

Some of the most successful early Argonauts—gold seekers—took little more on their quests than a tin wash pan in which to separate gold from earth, while others felt more comfortable outfitting themselves like L. L. Bean models. Ultimately, what you take with you, what you absolutely need, depends on you and, to a certain degree, on your experience as a writer. The following are suggestions.

PROVISIONS

We recommend that in addition to writing implements you include a loose-leaf notebook for doing the exercises and a bound notebook to serve as a log-book for recording your reactions and experiences as you do the exercises. These are by no means essential, and if acquiring them or using them deters you in any way, leave them behind. You may find later, however, that you would like a more organized and systematic way of dealing with the exercises. The notebook and logbook can serve well.

Use the logbook to record your efforts to complete the exercises, as well as your impressions and responses, in the way that some of the early prospectors recorded their prospecting adventures and findings, and the way that scientists record the conditions and outcomes of their experiments and doctors chart their patients' progress and setbacks. By doing this, you force yourself to stand back a little and think about what you've written and how you wrote it. In the long run, this logbook may be even more valuable to you than the exercises themselves.

While you can include anything you consider useful in the logbook, we suggest that you include the following:

1. Date and time you attempted the exercise
2. Where you were when you did the exercise
3. The name of the exercise
4. The amount of continuous time you spent on the exercise
5. The outcome of the exercise, including:
   a. your initial reaction to the exercise after reading it
   b. difficulties you encountered in doing the exercise
   c. discoveries you made while doing the exercise
   d. ideas that occurred to you for further writing

Items 1 through 4 are not particularly important, but recording these items can supply a sense of order, and they're easy enough to jot down. Item 5 is the crux of the logbook, though. Completing this item may take you even longer than completing the exercise.

The following illustrates a student's work on an exercise from the "Around the House" section of the book and his reaction in his logbook to that work and to the exercise itself:

Dave's Start on "Baggage" Exercise

Around the time I was ten, my mother asked me to pack for myself for a family trip up the coast. Early into the second day it became apparent that I had left behind all but one pair of underwear in the top drawer back home. How come we didn't make a detour to do some underwear shopping, I don't know. Each evening before bed I took off my size 22 J. C. Penney briefs to air them by the window. My brother and visiting cousin thought this was pretty funny. They didn't pack for themselves . . . yet. Underwear always tops my list of things to bring on vacation. . . .

Dave's Logbook Entry

DATE/TIME:	*July 19, 1999, 5:00 P.M.*
PLACE:	*Duck, NC*
NAME OF EXERCISE:	*"Baggage"*
AMOUNT OF TIME:	*About Thirty Minutes*

Outcomes
Reactions/Responses to Doing the Exercise:
I need more thoughts into spinning a metaphor out of forgetting underwear.

Difficulties:
Couldn't get going on the "Excavating" part of the exercise. I can't really remember much emotion with my trip—do I make it up?

Discoveries:
I don't like looking for psychological baggage.

Ideas for Further Writing:
1. *The nagging feeling you experience before leaving that something is left behind.*
2. *Why do I usually take so much underwear on a trip?*
3. *Taking a road trip with brother and cousin and the dynamics between the three of us and the parents.*

The following student worked on a couple of exercises from "Around the House" for an hour and decided to react to both of them together in the log sheet that follows his starts:

Mike's Start on "Folk Remedies"
To cure forgetfulness, place two garlic bulbs in a glass of Listerine and shake. Next, stand on a stack of encyclopedias and drink the concoction while squeezing your wallet.

Mike's Start on "The Note Read, 'There Are More Where These Came From'"
Mad,
Went to the playground; back in a half-hour.

8:00, Mike

Mad,
Money is on the coffee table. You are on empty. Sorry, I had to rush home with ice cream.

Call me, Mike

Mad,
Where are the August Safeway coupons? Check #861—Who and how much? Who's got Max tonight?

Mike

Mad,
While you were out, all of your friends called. They are all having serious crises that require long telephone conversations. They all want you to call back immediately.

Mike

Mike's Start on "Product Warnings"

Common Warnings:

- *Harmful if swallowed*
- *Use only in well-ventilated areas*
- *The Surgeon General has determined that smoking is dangerous to your health*
- *Smoking by pregnant women may cause low birth weight*
- *Induce vomiting if swallowed*

New Combinations:

- *Swallowing may induce vomiting in pregnant women*

Mike's Logbook Entry

DATE/TIME: *June 8, 1994, 3–4 P.M.*
PLACE: *Deli Parking Lot/In Car*
NAME OF EXERCISE: *"Folk Remedies," "The Note Read, 'There Are More Where These Came From,'" and "Product Warnings"*
AMOUNT OF TIME: *One Hour*

Outcomes

Reactions/Responses to Doing the Exercise:
I enjoyed them—which surprised me.

Difficulties:
I found it difficult to get started and to keep going, but I did.

Discoveries:
I am creatively stunted and need serious work—ha!

Ideas for Further Writing:
Product Warnings for major life decisions. How would these be given? Would you have to sign off that you had received the warnings? Would you then be prohibited from later complaining about your car, family, job, and so on?

As you can see from these first two logbook entries, there's no right or wrong way to keep a logbook. Although both Dave and Mike are beginning writers, Dave may be taking his writing more seriously at this point than Mike takes his. Yet each has made some interesting and potentially useful comments that may help them develop as writers. Dave feels pleased with the "voice" in this piece, but is beginning to question his unwillingness to examine psychological and emotional areas in his writing. Mike may seem to laugh off or dismiss the work he has done, but he does allow himself to admit he enjoyed writing—an important impetus for doing more—and he comes up with an intriguing idea for another piece.

The next exercise start and sample logbook entry were completed by a writer with somewhat more experience than either Dave or Mike:

Toni's Start on "At the Dinner Table"

"Dinner's ready, everyone!" my mother yelled out from the kitchen.

"Oh, joy," my brother said, turning the page of the detective novel he was reading.

"That means you, too, mister!" my mother yelled as if she could see him still lying there.

I put one more piece in the puzzle I was putting together—the cherry on the top of an ice-cream sundae two smiling teenage girls were sharing—and stepped back from the card table to survey my work. I had done this puzzle at least twenty times since I bought it with my allowance money two weeks before, but each time I put it together, the world in it that I had assembled seemed new and almost magical.

"Let's go, secret agent No. 14," my brother said, up from the couch now and nudging me toward the dining room where, per usual, we'd find our stepfather sitting at the head of the table waiting for my mother to serve him.

I took my place quietly and watched as my mother heaped spoonfuls of the creamy tuna noodle casserole she had made on his plate. This was a new recipe. We found it in one of her magazines earlier in the day, and I knew she was nervous about whether he would like it. Some of the ingredients—crunchy onion bits and angel hair noodles, for example—were pretty exotic, at least as far as our household was concerned.

I could see that none of us were going to get served until he tried it. I thought of the ice-cream sundae I was building in the other room, listened to my brother clear his throat suggestively, and concentrated on not letting my stomach growl. Slowly my stepfather's fork made its way to his plate. The only thing I disliked more than watching him eat was waiting for him to begin. Then he put down his fork and adjusted his water glass while we all waited. . . .

Toni's Logbook Entry

DATE/TIME:	March 3, 1999, 1:30 P.M.
PLACE:	Ledo's Pizza Place
NAME OF EXERCISE:	"At the Dinner Table"
AMOUNT OF TIME:	45 Minutes

Outcomes

Reactions/Responses to Doing the Exercise:
I thought this was going to be a tough exercise because I couldn't immediately remember any particular family meal. They all kind of blurred together.

Difficulties:
It took me a long time (about 10 minutes) to get an angle on the exercise before I could really start writing.

Discoveries:
I finally suddenly remembered this meal that I just knew was absolutely typical of all our meals together. I remembered that my stepfather never cooked—never even washed a dish—and it kind of irritated me to think about him.

Ideas for Further Writing:
I think it would be interesting to imagine my stepfather actually trying to prepare a meal for my brother and myself—from our point of view at that age. Maybe I could write a truly fictional piece where I focused on his awkwardness as a chef. It's hard even to imagine him setting the table—the slim silverware in those big awkward hands of his.

Your own log entries may be as detailed and analytical as Toni's, or they may be shorter, like Dave's or Mike's. Our experience has been that the more writers write, the more developed their logbook journal entries become. But, as we have seen, even shorter, early entries can provide a novice writer with valuable clues for future exploration.

Optional Provisions

Many writers and other creative people also use journals to jot down ideas and observations, as well as diaries to record reflections and experiences, and these can serve as valuable sources of material for stories, poems, and essays. Some writers also find it useful to keep several notecards around for moments of inspiration. In addition to being very portable (they fit in a shirt pocket or wallet), notecards can be organized in a variety of ways, including by color.

PROSPECTING TOOLS

Beyond a desire to write and a willingness to freely explore your imagination, all that you need to get started are a few simple prospecting tools to help you dislodge material from your imagination—the picks, shovels, and sluice boxes of the writing process. Many of the tools we describe in this section perform basically the same function: they loosen up or shake up or knock down material from memory and imagination, in a fashion similar to the action of picks, shovels, and dynamite. The idea in using these tools, and, indeed, with this entire book, is to free up your thinking processes and imagination. No claim we make in this book is any more certain than the claim that you have within you 24-karat experiences, memories, and imaginings. Which tools you use to get at this internal gold is simply a matter of what you and your sensibility feel most comfortable using. While some of the exercises will prompt you to use specific tools (these will be highlighted in **bold**), we suggest that you try them all at least once or twice in the course of completing the exercises. As anyone who has used tools knows, the right tool can make the difference between a day and a week of work.

Freewriting

As the name of this technique suggests, **freewriting** is a way of freely jotting down whatever occurs to you. At its freest, freewriting is simply writing anything and everything that comes to mind with no regard for meaning, significance, or topic. The point of doing this is to allow your unconscious to pour its beauty, uniqueness, and wildness into your writing. Variations on freewriting make it less free but perhaps more effective for certain situations.

Timed freewriting imposes a time limit for the freewriting, say five to ten minutes. During this period, you should write continuously, again without regard to what you are writing. If you can't think of anything and are about to stop, simply repeat the last thing you wrote or repeat a phrase you used before, for example "I'm thinking about, I'm thinking about, I'm thinking about" or "I can't think, I can't think, I can't think," until you come up with something else. The idea is just to write continuously for a period of time you prescribe for yourself. The following is an example of two minutes of timed freewriting:

> freewriting freewriting what's free about freewriting pencils? pencils are cheap who uses a pencil anymore? can't think of anything can't think of anything except the smell of pencil shavings the way it takes me back to grade school fond memories but which ones specifically something about pencil shavings that smell the smell of promise the unopened box of crayons the new notebooks such hopeful things but by the second week everything's written in tattered the crayons broken the compass and scissors lost pencil shavings do that to me can't think of anything can't think of anything except the Mets what about the Mets? who cares I don't know much about baseball except it makes me tense the psychology of pitchers and batters the waiting the waiting and scratching waiting and scratching what an image adults do this waiting and scratching.

Focused freewriting takes off on specific words or ideas and returns to the words or ideas periodically. Again, the idea is to write continuously without evaluation, but in this case with some effort to generally focus on a topic, subject, or theme. With focused freewriting, you may digress or take off from your topic as long as your digression is interesting to you; however, when you run out of things to say about the digression, return to the words or ideas with which you started. The following illustrates how focused freewriting can move back and forth from the concept of "vacations":

Vacations

Time away from something less than completely desirable. I remember our vacations to the lake—Lake Mohawk . . . a very green lake that used to be called Lake Cow but was renamed for marketing purposes. Wanted to attract more kids. The great thing about Lake Mohawk was that it had a high water slide and a pier in the middle also a long rope that swung out over the water. The first time I swung out and dropped into that water I was shocked first by how cold it was and then by how deep I'd fallen. Didn't know which way was up and at first swam down thinking it was up and realized in panic. . . . Vacations are times spent in alternative realities. Shakespeare's characters had important revelations in the woods, which were always enchanted. Vacation. Vacate. Make empty. To vacate a building. Motel vacancy. To vacate our senses. A vacation from sense. A vacation from despair. . . . Vacant.

Notice how the writer of the above example allows herself to explore how Lake Mohawk got its name and even to bring in Shakespeare's romances. Then, finally, she brings the freewriting back to the concept and meaning of "vacation."

Freewriting can be used at any stage of the writing process to shake loose material in your memory and imagination. It can be used alone or in combination with the other techniques we're about to discuss.

Brainstorming

You may already be familiar with this writing tool as a problem-solving technique used in many other contexts. What **brainstorming** shares with freewriting and some other techniques we will discuss is, again, the absence of self-judgment or evaluation. Brainstorming works best when used in conjunction with specific prompt questions. In the initial stages of a typical problem-solving situation, a question related to the problem is posed and solutions are solicited. All solutions—even the wildest and most bizarre—are tentatively accepted and recorded. After *all* conceivable solutions have been provided, then, and only then, should evaluation of each suggestion begin. As a simple example, let's say your back door tends to swing in the wind because the latch doesn't work. Brainstorming among members of the family, the following creative solutions are offered:

1. Use a bungee cord to hold it closed.
2. Call the locksmith.
3. Use two huge magnets.
4. Strap it back with nylon stockings.
5. Take off the door.

6. Block the wind.
7. Have somebody stand there and hold it closed.
8. Stick gerbils under the door.
9. Invite neighbors over for a door-closing party.
10. Pile recyclables in front of the door.

While the above example of brainstorming involves solutions to a material problem, this same technique can be used in writing to generate and explore ideas. Imagine writing about a couple of the unlikely solutions listed above, not in an effort to solve a material problem but as a way of getting started:

Idea for a Story
The door was held open by a pair of nylon stockings. Something was definitely wrong. She was sitting in the kitchen drinking a Coke and twirling a pair of scissors the way cowboys used to twirl their Colt 45s. . . .

Idea for an Essay
The mechanical world and I have had a testy relationship. When things break, I tend to get emotional, and the mechanical world couldn't care less. I got so frustrated with the door that kept banging open and closed despite my efforts to make it stop that I called all my neighbors and told them to come over. I told them I was having a party, a party just to celebrate that door, that wonderful door. My best friends understood; the door, I suspect, didn't.

Idea for a Poem
The back door bangs shut
as often as it swings open
but the latter I hear, the latter
unnerves. I tie it closed
with a pair of nylon stockings.
The new silence also
unnerves as crisp as something
unearned. . . .

Listing
In some ways very similar to freewriting and brainstorming, **listing** is a popular and fun way of establishing categories and filling them with creative examples.

The listing activity uses questions, prompts, or categories, either given or created, to generate items both predictable and surprising, tame and wild, colorful and drab. Listing provides an inviting structure within which creative momentum can mount and produce some surprising results, as the following student example illustrates:

Prompt: *Reasons I never wear green*
1. *It clashes with my eyes.*
2. *I blend in with the grass.*
3. *I feel like a clown.*
4. *I'm often mistaken for an after-dinner mint.*
5. *It reminds me of the money I don't have.*
6. *It clashes with my eyes.*
7. *I look like I'm dead.*
8. *I faint.*
9. *It makes me feel Irish.*
10. *It suggests that I lack experience.*
11. *I feel like a clown.*
12. *Everything I eat tastes like lime.*
13. *It clashes with my eyes.*
14. *None of my perfumes match.*

Notice that this writer repeats ideas when she feels momentarily stuck for something new. We suggest using listing in several exercises and supply prompts and questions to help you get started. You should also consider using lists in exercises that don't specifically ask for them, if the material seems suitable.

Clustering

For those who are more visually oriented and who like to draw and doodle, **clustering** may be a very productive writing tool (see the example on the following page). Invented by Gabriele Rico, the author of *Writing the Natural Way*, clustering involves drawing circles around words and phrases and connecting them to other circles with related words and phrases. This is a very intuitive and recursive process that shows you how ideas branch and grow and permutate. The sample creates a cluster from the word *green*, the subject of the last exercise.

Notice how each balloon in the cluster becomes the beginning or nucleus of another cluster. The centers of the clusters and associated clusters can be combined in a variety of ways to begin poems, stories, or essays.

Free Association

Developed and made popular by Freudian psychoanalysts, **free association** is a technique for getting at what Freudians would call repressed material in the unconscious. To free associate means to say the first thing that comes to your mind when presented with a word, a phrase, or an object. Freud discovered that when his patients slipped and said something that sounded like a simple mistake, often the mistake highlighted or pointed to a complex of some kind. This is the origin of the expression "Freudian slip." In writing,

Sample Cluster

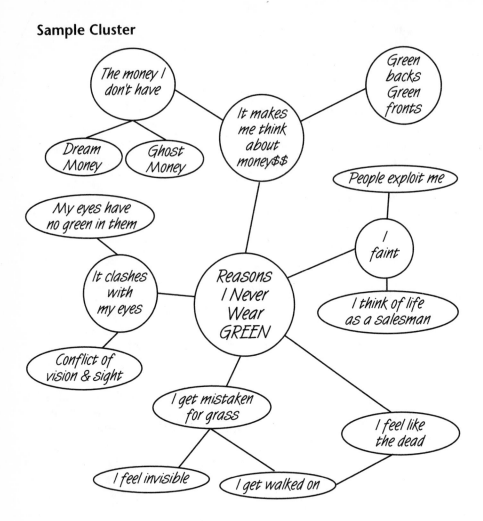

this technique can help you generate some surprising material when you keep it up for a few minutes, free associating from one word to the next. When used by an analyst, free association begins with the analyst saying one word and the patient responding immediately with the first word that comes to mind. The analyst then provides another word, and the patient repeats the process with that word, and so on. When the patient responds with something significant or unusual, the analyst may stop the free associations to talk about specific responses to see where they lead.

In the context of a writing exercise, there is of course no analyst to supply words; however, free associating in a chain or sequence alone can also have the effect of dredging up surprising material.

For example, let's see where free associating took one student who was just starting on the "Checking Out the Checkout Line" exercise:

mayonnaise mustard mustache circus clouds billowing ballet light face sponge noon heroine Lincoln snake tide evening moon

Notice how the above sequence of free associations leaps around, at times almost making sense, but ultimately creating a very individual psychic trail. No two people would produce the same sequence. These words, while seemingly unrelated, came from the same mind. The connections remain to be explored and used by the writer. The writer may choose to freewrite or list possible connections between words she has free associated, or she may begin a story, essay, or poem that incorporates several of the words and their relationship.

Puzzles, Games, and Computers

In addition to those that you already possess, there are many other valuable writing tools that themselves use other tools or things or documents that have already been created. The possibilities for generating writing ideas using computer software, for example, are probably limitless, and the last few years have produced many programs aimed specifically at writing and the various steps in the writing process. Word games such as Scrabble, Boggle, Twenty Questions, and Ad Libs can be used directly or can be adapted to help you generate ideas for beginning. The following list of tools is by no means exhaustive, and we encourage you to look for other tools that can help you generate exciting writing ideas.

Puzzling Crosswords. Even if you don't have a lot of success with that crossword puzzle in the *New York Times,* you can use it or other crossword puzzles to help you generate writing ideas. This technique requires that you give up on "their" solution and use the structure of the puzzle to help you find your solutions.

You can use this tool simply to come up with random words, or you can use it to develop one of the exercises in this book. To do the latter, simply write the name of the exercise (for example, "Baggage") above any unworked crossword puzzle from any source. Next, ignoring the puzzle's clues, simply fill in only the vertical elements or the horizontal elements of the puzzle with words related to the exercise—or any other words—that fit in the spaces. (Do not try to use both vertical and horizontal elements to make crosswords. This will drive you nuts, and it's not the point anyway, as you will see.) Then, simply list all the words you used to fill the blanks in the puzzle, mix and match them, combine and modify them, and use them in the piece you're working on, as appropriate.

The writer who filled in the crossword puzzle below came up with this start on a story:

> When the new contractors opened the wall to look at the wiring, they discovered several empty beer cans between the studs. No wonder the estimate was so good from the first electricians. Everything had to be ripped out and done over.
>
> The new contractor, a guy named Allen, said, "Well, don't think too hard on him. It's not an easy life being a wire man."
>
> "Does that mean you condone this?"
>
> "No, ma'am," he said. "In fact, my whole crew's in AA—though I'm not supposed to tell you that."

Sample Crossword Puzzle

Home Contractors
Judy Andersen

¹R	²O	³O	⁴F		⁵P	⁶A	⁷I	⁸N	⁹T		¹⁰S	¹¹I	¹²N	¹³K
¹⁴M	E	S	S		¹⁵D	R	A	I	N		¹⁶D	E	C	K
¹⁷T	H	I	¹⁸S	I	S	A	E	S	T	¹⁹I	M	A	T	E
²⁰M	O	R	T	A	R			²¹D	R	I	L	L		
²²B	R	U	S	H		²³L	²⁴A	B	O	R		²⁵S	²⁶A	²⁷W
²⁸T	A	R		²⁹C	O	S	T	S		³⁰S	L	A	B
		³¹N	³²O	I	S	E		³³B	E	A	M	S
	³⁴A	³⁵G	O	O	D	S	C	³⁶H	³⁷E	D	U	L	E
³⁸N	A	I	L	S		³⁹T	O	O	L	S		
⁴⁰P	R	E	P		⁴¹S	⁴²T	U	D	S		⁴³B	⁴⁴I	⁴⁵D
⁴⁶S	U	B		⁴⁷S	N	A	K	E		⁴⁸C	⁴⁹O	A	T	S
	⁵⁰L	⁵¹E	V	E	L		⁵²P	R	I	M	E	R
⁵³A	⁵⁴L	O	T	O	F	⁵⁵B	⁵⁶A	D	W	I	R	I	N	G
⁵⁷L	E	A	K		⁵⁸G	L	A	Z	E		⁵⁹B	E	E	R
⁶⁰S	A	S	H		⁶¹P	U	T	T	Y		⁶²W	O	O	D

Word Strings. Choose one word related to your exercise and write another word beginning with the last letter of the first word that relates to your exercise—however remotely—and keep this up until you've generated at least ten words. For example, let's say you're working on the "Crossing Relationship Boundaries" exercise, and you have chosen to explore your relationship with your brother. You, in fact, begin with the word *brother:*

> *brother ridiculous selfish hearty youthful lively yearning grouchy yet tame eager relentless sad*

More than likely, in the course of completing the string, you will come up with some ideas that might not have occurred to you otherwise. Try to incorporate some of these words and concepts in your initial writing efforts.

Using Your Computer

There are many computer programs on the market now that address the various steps in the writing process. Some packages have prewriting software that allows you to automatically match nouns and relevant verbs and create ideas and word chains. Although no program can substitute for your memories and imagination, it can be fun to experiment with the software. But even if you have access only to word-processing software with a dictionary and thesaurus, you can use a computer to generate writing ideas.

Computer Thesaurus. Choose a word from the title of an exercise or a word that you came up with while freewriting, brainstorming, or engaging in one of the other prewriting techniques described in this section, and look it up in the computer thesaurus. Next, draw up a list of synonyms and antonyms and use them to take you in different directions related to your subject. For example, let's say you're working on the "Neighborly and Unneighborly Neighbors" exercise and that you look up the word *neighbor* in the thesaurus. The following options appear:

> *abut*
> *acquaintance*
> *adjoin*
> *associate*
> *border*
> *connect*
> *flank*
> *friend*
> *skirt*

The concept of "flank" captures your imagination, so you look it up in the thesaurus, with the following result:

fringe
haunch
line
loin
quarter
verge on
wing

You are struck by the fact that *flank* can refer both to "side" in general and also to a side of meat in particular. You note several other terms for cuts of meat, such as *loin, wing,* and *haunch.* Your search through the thesaurus has resulted in a potentially interesting relationship between neighbors and butchery. This relationship could serve as the beginning of a story, poem, or essay. Notice, though, that other synonyms would lead in other directions. For example, you might just as well have chosen *skirt,* which might suggest another direction that the exercise about neighbors might take.

You can use a bound thesaurus as well with this approach, but you may lose some of the fluidity that a computer thesaurus provides.

Computer Dictionary. Purposely misspell any word related to one of the exercises to see what other words your internal computer dictionary offers. For example, let's say you are doing the "Quilting" exercise and misspell the word *corduroy* as "coduroy." Our computer dictionary asked us to consider the following options besides the correct spelling of *corduroy:*

Calder
caldera
cantery
cedar
colder
cooter
couture

The word *corduroy* likely derives from the proper name *Corduroy,* possibly from the French for ribbon or road (*corde*) of the king (*roi*). *Calder* is a modern artist known for his large mobiles. *Caldera* is the expanded vent of a volcano, and the word derives from *caldron.* Down South, to *cooter* means to loiter or to be idle, as in "Stop cootering and get busy." *Couture* refers to sewing and dressmaking. These remotely related words could be imaginatively incorporated into a poem about corduroy:

And way back in the corner of the closet, a pair
of brown corduroy pants, the king of style
when I was in college, now as quaint
in its lapsed modernity
as a Calder mobile cootering
in the winds of artistic promise . . .

Resistance as a Tool

For many of you, refraining from judging your initial exploratory writing efforts may be the hardest exercise. If you find this to be the case, we recommend that, in writing, you "talk back" to your inclinations to judge the outcomes of the exercises. Because most of us are accustomed to writing to someone else's expectations—even in the early stages of the writing process—you may experience some discomfort or resistance in your efforts at getting started. Acknowledging that discomfort and talking back to it, preferably in your logbook, is one sure way of overcoming it, and also of generating even more material. The following example taken from a student's logbook illustrates what can come from talking back to "the critic within," that evaluative faculty that we all possess for good reasons, but that can short-circuit creativity if invoked too early:

I feel funny doing this so-called freewriting. It seems wrong to write this way. I was always taught to use an outline and know what you're going to say. Ms. Wilson in sixth grade was a stickler for outlines. God, everything was Roman numeralized. Numeralized?? Wonder if that's a word. Don't Numeralize me. . . . but then, the idea is to come up with things to say and write about, so how can it be wrong? It just feels funny, like running on at the mouth, out of control . . . control is so important, but should it always be?

Notice how in talking back to the evaluative faculty, the writer above actually generates some ideas for writing about an early experience, discovers an interesting word, and acknowledges the importance of control. So long as you keep this kind of internal dialogue going on paper, the interplay between your imagination and the act of writing will continue.

Pay particular attention any time you encounter resistance while trying to do the exercises. While you may conclude that your difficulties doing an exercise are due to something you lack—for example, skill, creativity, or will—or that this book lacks, it's possible that the exercise is dredging up powerful though uncomfortable material from your subconscious, such as a memory, guilt, or a fear. It is at such points, however, that you may have stunning imaginative breakthroughs.

Notice in the example above that the writer questions the importance of control. If the writer has never before acknowledged this tendency in herself, the acknowledgment here may come as a revelation and clear the way for a freer and more honest engagement with her imagination.

In our workshops, when students complain that the exercises are difficult, weird, irrelevant, and so on, they nevertheless produce exciting results when they push themselves to complete them. In fact, those who have complained the most are among those who have turned in the most extraordinary exercises. This shouldn't surprise anyone, because to complain about anything is to bring focus and strong feelings to bear on the object of complaint. These are two qualities of great value in the creative process. As teachers, we have come to regard moaning about the exercises as a healthy prelude to exciting discoveries.

Using a Combination of Tools

Probably no single tool that we've mentioned will be adequate to dig up or dredge up or unclog or dislodge all the imaginative material that you can bring to an exercise, since each tool tends to work best with specific facets of our minds. Therefore, we encourage you to use a variety of tools and to become adroit at shifting. Begin with **freewriting,** shift to **clustering,** switch over to **brainstorming** or **listing,** look up a word on the **computer thesaurus,** and so forth, as the following student example illustrates:

I don't know what to write I don't know what to write cellophane what is cellophane it's like a cello and profanity cellophane fascinates me six wonderful things about cellophane	**Freewriting**
1. it's transparent	
2. it leaves no scars	
3. it attracts jelly fish	**Listing**
4. it tastes like chicken	
5. it's good for keeping corpses fresh	
6. it's better for you than iceberg lettuce	
Imagine, cellophane is used to cover iceberg lettuce and is probably better for you than the lettuce	**Focused Freewriting**

Iceberg lettuce gets a bad rap. How to improve the
reputation of iceberg lettuce

Brainstorming

1. Go on TV. Iceberg lettuce does a body good.
2. Have a contest to name uses of iceberg lettuce.
3. Have a celebrity represent iceberg lettuce. Who?
   a. George Hamilton
   b. Heather Locklear
   c. Cher
4. Make iceberg lettuce the hero of some kind of
   drama.
5. Microwave iceberg lettuce and put salt on it.
6. Create an iceberg the size of Toledo in the shape
   of a head of lettuce.

Focused Freewriting

But eating iceberg lettuce makes me feel empty.
It's like the opposite of eating. Popcorn does the
same thing to me as does watermelon . . .
beginning of poem

Computer Thesaurus

Loving her was like dining on
iceberg lettuce: it seemed healthy ⟵⟶ hale
and good but it was nothing   hearty
less than nothing   vigorous
it made me hungrier.   robust

Loving her was like dining on
iceberg lettuce: it seemed robust
and good but it was nothing.
Less than nothing.
It made me hungrier.

Notice how the writer began with an **unfocused freewriting** that led him
to the word *cellophane*. He decided to do **listing** on this discovered word and
then moved to a **focused freewriting** on iceberg lettuce, which was a discovery from his **listing** activity. He **brainstormed** on iceberg lettuce, and
after another brief **focused freewriting** began a poem that makes a surprising connection between iceberg lettuce and a relationship he had with a
woman. While the poem is clearly just a start, it is a golden start because by
giving his imagination the freedom and tools to wander, the writer has
tapped into something original, fresh, and expressive.

WHAT FORM SHOULD YOU CHOOSE?

There are stories that should have been poems and essays that should have been stories. Likewise, there are those who think of themselves as story writers who show much more talent for poetry. Playwright Edward Albee, author of *Who's Afraid of Virginia Woolf?* wrote poetry for years before discovering and deciding that he was better at writing plays. A few creative writers have shown nearly equal skill and talent in more than one form of creative writing: Robert Penn Warren, poetry and fiction; Anton Chekhov, short stories and plays; Alice Walker, Joyce Carol Oates, and John Updike, fiction and poetry; Joan Didion, fiction and essays; Maya Angelou, creative nonfiction and poetry.

If you are a beginning writer, it's probably a good idea to remain open to your own potential for writing in these various forms—even if you believe you have decided to write in only one form. Likewise, it's probably a good idea to remain open to the form that your beginning efforts with these exercises will ultimately take.

Many excellent books have been written that define and characterize good stories, poems, and essays. Because this book focuses on the ideas for beginning any piece of creative writing, such discussions are beyond its scope, however. We nevertheless include below some factors that might go into your decision to write a poem, story, or essay from the ideas generated from the exercises in this book.

Consider Writing a Poem from an Exercise if

1. The sounds of the words and the language engage you as much as the meaning.
2. The sentences develop into distinctive rhythms and patterns of repetition.
3. The images are particularly strong.
4. The sentences do not refer to a specific time or place.

Notice how the following Nugget from "Customs and the Customary" lends itself to a kind of lyric poetry, though it may well have gone in another direction:

My House

In my house you must remove your shoes
and place them on your hands. Once
conversation begins, you may drop one
at a time to punctuate what
you are saying. In my house

you must try to draw a picture of me
and tell me why this is how you see me.
(All such efforts hang on the Great Wall, signed
and dated.) Here, no mention is ever made
of presidents, dead or living. You are expected
to rise when I rise, place a hand on my shoulder
and walk with me to the bathroom. In my house
the most venerable custom is the great dance
that takes place upon leaving: we embrace
as in a tango, re-trace our steps and conversations
and move out of the house, where I stop
turn, and you
are gone.

DOROTHY NIMS

The first line describes an ancient Asian custom, and the writer could have developed a story or even an essay about the conflicts or problems this custom has caused her. However, in the very next image of putting the shoes on the hands, the writer enters another realm, both surreal and imagistic and certainly non-literal. The repetition of "In my house" draws attention to the language and away from narrative, as do other words, such as "punctuate" and the rhyme "embrace" and "re-trace." Whatever the writer's initial intentions, this piece found one form and home in poetry.

Consider Writing a Story from an Exercise if

1. The question of what happens next becomes paramount.
2. Characters and their relationships have become focal points of your exercise.
3. Scene description and dialogue emerge as significant elements.

The following Nugget from "The Backpack" has potential for both an essay about dating and single mothers or a story about what happens when one single mother tries to put off the inevitable disclosure:

> Megan hadn't meant to mislead Alan when the plastic dinosaur had fallen out of her purse. It was just that she had seen his office, with its clutter of political cartoons, his hanging rubber stork, pink slinky and other miscellaneous anti-establishment toys, and wanted him to know that she wasn't buying into the system either. So, when Alan picked it up and said "Cool" and handed the

Brachiosaurus back to her with a new glimmer of recognition in his eye, she hadn't found it necessary to tell him that the toy belonged to her son, and that she had only this morning rescued it from under his car seat.

Mostly she was relieved that her purse hadn't been dumped in front of him the year before when there would have been baby wipes and a spare pacifier mixed in with the usual wallet, checkbook and keys. She decided now, today, was definitely a better time.

ANGELIN DONOHUE

In this passage, the careful description of character and the establishment of suspense suggest that this material might be best used in a story. We are left wondering "what happened?"—a question that is the hallmark of narrative fiction.

Consider Writing an Essay from an Exercise if
1. A lesson or moral or argument begins to emerge.
2. You want to prove or illustrate some point you touched on or discovered.
3. You want to explore the significance of an actual event.

The writer of the following beginning from the exercise "Holding On and Letting Go" seems to be in search of some truth about human behavior:

Six A.M. I've finished shaving, bathing, talcing, fumigating, combing, shirting and slacking. All that remains is socking and, of course, shoeing. I pull open what I have come to think of as "Pandora's Drawer," not because of what might fly out of it but because of what I rarely find: two dark socks that match and that do not have holes in them. It is a fine day that meets both criteria. I have entertained the notion of throwing all these socks out and buying two dozen pairs of the same shade of black (Black, I have learned through my socks, is a Platonic ideal. Black no more exists than the tooth fairy or immortality among mortals), but throwing them all out doesn't make sense, for there are, in this drawer from hell, a few intact matching pairs. But that still doesn't explain why I don't throw out the socks with holes in them. Every morning I see coins of flesh peeking like closed eyes from these socks, but instead of throwing them out, I put them right back in the drawer where I am just as likely to do this again.

I have a Ph.D. in economics. My mother did not raise a fool. My wife did not marry one. Why can't I throw these holey socks out?

HAKI WANZO

In his exploration of his tendency to hold on to his holey socks, Haki Wanzo reflects upon how this behavior is in conflict with his otherwise sensible and adult behaviors. While his wife and mother are briefly mentioned, Haki is clearly the subject of the piece, a sign that an essay format is probably the right way to go here. Finally, the question he ends with— What is the significance of my action?—seems most naturally answered or tackled in an essay.

Whether you end up pursuing a specific idea from one of the exercises in a poem, story, or essay, there is no law that says you cannot go back and try it out in another form, or in all forms. The advantage you have over Michelangelo is that you are not limited to discrete slabs of marble. The material you have generated from the exercises need not be thrown away when one form doesn't work but instead can be recast into a form that pleases you.

Around the House

Why I Will Not Get Out of Bed

Most of us have days when the world outside our bedroom seems too difficult to face. We skip school, call in sick, put off our errands until tomorrow, and spend the rest of the day feeling at once guilty and relieved as life generally goes on quite well without us.

Many view the decision to spend the day in bed as a passive choice, something we give in to when we lack the necessary physical or emotional energy to do much else. But it takes energy not to function in the way that is expected of us, to take a day off from the rhythm of our lives and spend time alone with only our inner resources for company. This exercise asks you to explore the reasons for making such a choice, to examine the forces that make you wish you could stay in bed certain mornings.

Panning Instructions

1. Brainstorm all the reasons you can think of for not getting out of bed. What is it about your day that you don't want to face? Get into your most negative frame of mind to imagine every possible thing that is wrong and might go wrong out there in the world.

2. Start a poem, story, or essay in which you justify your decision to stay in bed by including as many of the reasons you have come up with as possible.

Excavating Instructions

Sometimes we have trouble getting out of bed not because we're avoiding what is waiting for us but because we're avoiding what is not waiting for us. We may have trouble getting out of bed when someone we care about has moved away or died or when an emotion we have come to count on to make our life feel complete has faded. Getting out of bed then becomes a metaphor for facing a loss that we may not be ready to confront.

Begin a poem, story, or essay in which you explore an emotional reason for not getting out of bed. Robert Jackson, for example, is slowed down by the news of his death (see below). Notice the way James Tate builds to his revelation in "Why I Will Not Get Out of Bed" (page 28), but ultimately saves the revelation for the final lines.

 NUGGETS

From the beginning of an essay

The first thing I heard this morning when the clock radio went off was the news that I had been put to death in the gas chamber in Tallahassee, Florida.

This news was being reported because the man with my name—an admittedly common name—had spent a record number of years on death row, something like thirty-five years or maybe forty years, I don't know. The point is, what I heard when that radio went off was "Robert Jackson was put to death this morning at 5:03 A.M."

My wife heard it too, and her first reaction was to say, "Good, guess you don't have to go to work." But it wasn't my first reaction, though I didn't in fact want to get out of bed. It set me back, hearing this. It made me want to pull the covers over my head and just spend the day thinking about my life.

ROBERT JACKSON

Why I Will Not Get Out of Bed

I can't go down the hall
To see if she's survived
Another night,
To see if her will is stronger
Than her cells.
The battle of the white and red
Rages.
There is no neutrality
Where there are feelings.
Yet on the battle grounds
I cannot fight for her,
Only watch
Each time she falters.
Uncover my soul and see
If there is a smile I can offer.
I have no bravery.
Multiply, divide, and conquer.
I cannot bear who wins.

PATTY SEATON

Why I Will Not Get Out of Bed

The sheets are holding me
prisoner: clever grabbers,
breath-stealers.
They think they're very funny
indeed.

If I put my foot out
the rug snarls and
seizes my ankles.
I'll be tossed
high into the hallway,
thrown in a heap at
the bottom of the stairs.

Mostly I hate the way
the kitchen smirks
and unhinges its jaws:
how it gorges on my sleep,
how it gags on my dreams.

LIZ ENAGONIO

 ARTIFACTS

Why I Will Not Get Out of Bed

My muscles unravel
like spools of ribbon:
there is not a shadow

of pain. I will pose
like this for the rest
of the afternoon,

for the remainder
of all noons. The rain
is making a valley

of my dim features.
I am in Albania,
I am on the Rhine.

It is autumn,
I smell the rain,
I see children running

through columbine.
I am honey,
I am several winds.

My nerves dissolve,
my limbs wither—
I don't love you.

I don't love you.

JAMES TATE

Holding On and Letting Go

Many of us have difficulty letting go of things that have lost their usefulness. Clothes that never fit take up a third of our closets; date books and desk calendars optimistically purchased to help us organize our days wait to be scribbled in; the rowing machine bought with the healthiest of intentions stands up in the back of the closet like a skeleton. We hold on to much of this stuff because to throw it out would be to acknowledge defeat or, worse, change.

Sometimes we have outgrown an old life in which barbells or crochet hooks made sense; sometimes that life never really fit us right in the first place. Hidden away for years, these dust collectors go public only when we sell them through the classifieds, donate them to charity, or turn them out on the lawn for a yard sale.

In places in which others find dustballs and fire hazards, a writer can discover gold. The following exercises are designed to help you spin gold out of some of your forgotten "collections."

Panning Instructions

1. Discover what you have difficulty letting go of by rummaging through your drawers, closets, refrigerator, and, of course, under the bed. If you have them, attics, garages, and basements can also be excellent discovery places as long as you don't become overwhelmed or, worse, start cleaning.

Anything you do not use or have not used for a long time counts. For example, one person may discover a cache of plastic L'eggs pantyhose "eggs" in the back of her drawer, while another person may find eight different brands of salsa in the refrigerator, some dating back to the Carter administration and home to green and purple colonies of fungi.

Brainstorm uses for any of your uncovered treasures. Try to come up with at least five uses, as in the example below.

What My Seventeen Pantyhose Eggs Are Good For
- Filling with stones and shaking to music
- Filling with water and throwing from my window at people who irritate me

- Hiding under a sleeping chicken to see what she does when she wakes up
- Sending as Easter gifts if I sent Easter gifts
- Rolling down the stairs all at once to see which one is fastest

2. Freewrite on reasons it is so hard to throw out or get rid of things that are no longer truly useful. Begin a poem, story, or essay that explores this difficulty, as Haki Wanzo does in his essay "Dark Holes" (see below).

Excavating Instructions

Often, things we are reluctant to throw out bring up memories of old relationships, places we have lived, or other lives we have led. For example, consider Mrs. Havisham's wedding dress in Charles Dickens's *Great Expectations* (see page 32). An accidental ashtray collection discovered under a kitchen sink might remind someone of the pain of quitting smoking or the life he had when he still smoked. Several well-worn pairs of size 5 black jeans might remind someone else of her life before she became pregnant with her first child.

Work on a story, poem, or personal essay that explores the emotions elicited by the things you discovered for the panning exercise.

NUGGETS

From the essay "Dark Holes"

Six A.M. I've finished shaving, bathing, talcing, fumigating, combing, shirting and slacking. All that remains is socking and, of course, shoeing. I pull open what I have come to think of as "Pandora's Drawer," not because of what might fly out of it but because of what I rarely find: two dark socks that match and that do not have holes in them. It is a fine day that meets both criteria. I have entertained the notion of throwing all these socks out and buying two dozen pairs of the same shade of black (Black, I have learned through my socks, is a Platonic ideal. Black no more exists than the tooth fairy or immortality among mortals), but throwing them all out doesn't make sense, for there are, in this drawer from hell, a few intact matching pairs. But that still doesn't explain why I don't throw out the socks with holes in them. Every morning I see coins of flesh peeking like closed eyes from these socks, but instead of throwing them out, I put them right back in the drawer where I am just as likely to do this again.

I have a Ph.D. in economics.

My mother did not raise a fool.
My wife did not marry one.
Why can't I throw these holey socks out?

HAKI WANZO

 ## ARTIFACTS

From the novel *Great Expectations*

She was dressed in rich materials—satins, and lace, and silks—all of white. . . . She had not quite finished dressing, for she had but one shoe on—the other was on the table near her hand—her veil was but half arranged, her watch and chain were not put on, and some lace for her bosom lay with those trinkets, and with her handkerchief, and gloves, and some flowers, and a prayer book, all confusedly heaped about the looking glass.

. . . But, I saw that everything within my view which ought to be white, had been white long ago, and had lost its lustre, and was faded and yellow. I saw that the bride within the bridal dress had withered like the dress, and like the flowers, and had no brightness left but the brightness of her sunken eyes.

CHARLES DICKENS

Yard Sale

Nothing has prepared us for the man
who knows the current world
market value of cut glass bowls
or the connoisseur of broken speakers.

We are shy and flattered they want
our things and amazed at the things
they want: a chipped drinking glass
with a frieze of pink babies, a chair
as dark and thin as Don Quixote.

Even the purple and blue cubist painting
that looked like the ragged birth of some animal
sells—and at a price much higher
than we imagined. "Say what you will
about realism," the buyer says, "color
is always in." But how to price

bone white cylinders with deckled lids
when we don't even know what they are,
how they work, where, in our lives,
they come from. And we wonder now
if we're letting go of something
valuable or important or just
lucky and mysterious, like tonsils.
Perhaps the life turned out
on the lawn is the one we should live—
the life within, the one we should sell.

A woman with a baby carriage full
of spatulas backs carefully down
our driveway. Say what we will
about realism, it's not a question
of how many more eggs she can turn.

Michael C. Smith

Furniture Movers

No matter how efficient we think we are—or aren't—as housekeepers, most of us have had the experience of finding something unexpected when moving furniture. Maybe a pacifier, once belonging to our now five-year-old, is unearthed from under a heavy couch. Or the lost first draft of an essay we wrote on gun control for a freshman composition class turns up behind the stereo when we take it in for repair. Whether we are moving furniture to change the configuration of a room or to change our lives far more dramatically by relocating, what is hidden by our furniture itself is only one of the surprises to which we open ourselves.

When we shift our furniture around, we are literally altering the way we will live our lives. While a chair facing a wall has fairly obvious connotations—someone's being punished!—a couch that once faced a television and now faces a bookcase may mean more than a casual observer would notice.

In the following exercises, you will explore ways that your furniture—and what is hidden in and under it—offers opportunity for creative discoveries.

Panning Instructions

1. Enlist the help of a roommate, spouse, or friend and move a piece of furniture that you cannot remember having ever moved, or at least cannot remember having moved in a long while. Bedroom dressers are good places to start. If you're a truly excellent housekeeper, you may have to resort to inching your refrigerator out from the wall. (Please do not sue us for back injuries!)

After you're finished counting and cataloging dustballs, look for unexpected discoveries. A dusty quarter counts; a ticket stub counts; even a carpet stain you had forgotten you had covered up with this piece of furniture counts. If you come up empty, try another piece of furniture.

2. Freewrite for ten minutes about your discoveries, speculating about their origins or significance. Or **freewrite** for ten minutes about how your new space feels to you. In what ways do you feel confined, freed up, new, odd?

3. Read over your freewrite and highlight the parts that stand out for you the most in some way. Begin a story, poem, or essay that focuses on these findings. Or begin a story, poem, or essay with a sentence or two that renders one of the feelings this new arrangement of furniture gives you. For example, "My body didn't know how to get settled. I never slept facing a window before."

☀☀ Excavating Instructions

Sometimes we move furniture before or after a major event in our lives has occurred. Divorce, the birth of a child, a roommate moving in or out—all can mean shifting our lives literally and figuratively. Think back to a time when such a change in your life was imminent and **freewrite** about the change, grounding your experience in the moving of furniture. Maybe your roommate took the coffee table with her, and you were left with a pile of magazines on the floor. Maybe you bought a CD rack at a yard sale to organize your fiancé's CD collection. Begin a story, poem, or essay that incorporates meaningful material from your freewrite.

☀ NUGGETS

From an essay in progress

Many years later we tried to recall the event that had signaled the end. We laughed, rather sadly I thought, at the years of friendship thrown away over an event so slight that it left not even a dent in our memories. Our laughter subsided into an uncomfortable silence while we pondered our youthful stupidity.

"Remember how cold it was in that house once we had packed everything up?" I said. "Seemed like every box we taped shut took the temperature down about five degrees." I took a sip of coffee and peered at her over the edge of my steaming cup.

"I remember," she said. Another pause. I waited anxiously for her to continue, but I wasn't good at these empty spaces in conversation; I felt obligated to fill them up.

"Do you know why I stacked all my boxes in the living room for a week before I moved out?" I asked. She shook her head and reached for the warmth of her own cup, which had sat untouched until now.

"I wanted you to see them every time you walked through the room. I suppose I wanted you to miss me while I was still there and know that it was all your fault."

GINGER MAZZAPICA

 ## ARTIFACTS

From the short story "Furniture Drift"

To what epoch the Kneales' coffee table belongs is a topic of heated debate these days. The striations, the dark and light lines which run diagonally across it, seem to put it in the Miocene, but the table's location, so near the sofa, indicates a much earlier date (Paleocene?). Dr. Ledgarde, professor of geology at Tufts, argues for the Miocene reading; he argues loud and long, often very late into the night, and Mr. Kneale had to ask him to leave once, when it was almost two in the morning and Mr. Kneale worried that the neighbors might call the police and complain about the noise. Ledgarde seeks, at times with an almost self-destructive obsession, the sort of discovery that made the Kneales' friend, Rick, a big shot. It was Rick's discovery that if all the furniture in the Kneales' house were pushed to the center of the living room, it would fit together without any gaps, and that maybe this is what the living room looked like at one time. The idea was met, at first, with silence. Mrs. Kneale broke the silence when she looked at Rick and said, "Can I get you anything from the kitchen while I'm up?"

Supporting evidence for the furniture drift theory came when the Kneales' precocious twelve-year-old, Jason, discovered a sub-carpet stratum of molten hardwood floor in the entry way while test drilling for mineral deposits. . . .

BARRY STOLTZ

Baggage

or every person who brags about spending a summer traveling around the country with nothing but a small backpack containing three pairs of socks and a camera, there is another person who packs an entire wardrobe for a two-week stay at a nearby beach. When we pack, we are forced to confront our essential natures. The classic worrier hides traveler's checks in three separate bags and memorizes his credit-card numbers in case they are stolen. The workaholic packs an extra battery-pack for her notebook computer. And the serious sightseer brings three different travel guides.

Still, we make mistakes, anticipating formal dinners only to wind up eating fast food. We forget that drugstores exist in other cities, and even other countries, and we scoop up handfuls of trial size bottles of shampoo and shaving cream and line our suitcases with them, only to take half of them back home again.

And no matter how well we think we've packed, most of us have had the experience of forgetting something as basic as a toothbrush or as important as the first page of a report for a business presentation.

Panning Instructions

1. Make a list of several items you have forgotten to pack for a vacation or business trip. Notice Joan Didion's "significant omission" in the excerpt from her essay "The White Album" (page 39).
2. Make a second list of items you have packed but didn't need or use once you got to your destination.
3. Make a third list of unlikely things either to pack or to forget to pack for a trip. For example, a list might begin the following way:

- A pink flamingo
- My first-grade report card
- A towel Mick Jagger wiped his forehead with

4. To help you begin to get started on a story, poem, or piece of creative nonfiction that takes off from these lists, try completing some of the following statements with truths, lies, or a combination of the two:

I opened my bag and was horrified that I had forgotten to pack
_____.

The _____ I packed proved totally useless.

I never thought that _____ would come in handy, but it sure did.

When I opened my suitcase, I was surprised to find I had packed
_____.

My _____ (mother, husband, sister, etc.) told me not to bring my
_____, but of course I didn't listen.

Excavating Instructions

Psychologists claim we all carry psychic "baggage" around with us—wounds from our childhoods, betrayals by ex-lovers. Make a list of some of the baggage you carry. For example, someone's list might begin the following way:

- Anger from that time my father grounded me for two weeks when I got caught shoplifting.
- Sadness from my mother's death.

Pack the story, poem, or essay that you began in Panning in one of these pieces of "baggage" by bringing that emotion to your writing. One way of doing this is to have the items you have either forgotten or remembered become metaphors for an enduring feeling. For an example of this, notice the way the character in the excerpt from Jud McClosky's short story (see below) packs electrical extension cords—perhaps because of his insecurity over losing touch with power.

NUGGETS

From the short story "The King's Gopher"

After tipping the bellhop, he turned to the task of unpacking the suitcase he had so meticulously packed nearly a week ago. The socks were rolled in little balls and lay nestled in the corner of the suitcase like dark eggs. There were the usual slacks, shirts and underwear, but there were also three electrical extension cords lined up in the satin pockets around the sides of the suitcase. From his many years of travel he had learned that there are never enough outlets in hotels, even though he rarely if ever needed to plug something in. He placed the extension cords in the same drawer with his belts.

He unpacked quickly because he was anxious to call the regional office to find out if Howard Winston, the vice president of marketing, had arrived. They weren't scheduled to meet until late the next day, but he liked to know where Winston was at all times. Even in New York, he would sometimes call Winston's secretary just to learn what he already knew, that he was tied up in some meeting or other. More than a hobby, tracking the executives was the only way he knew of getting a handle on his fear that he was losing touch with the power in the organization. It gave him a sense of control, and sometimes it gave him just enough information to allow him a night's sleep.

JUD MCCLOSKY

 ## ARTIFACTS

From the essay "The White Album"
TO PACK AND WEAR:
2 skirts
2 jerseys or leotards
1 pullover sweater
2 pair shoes
stockings
bra
nightgown, robe, slippers
cigarettes
bourbon
bag with:
    shampoo
    toothbrush and paste
    Basis soap
    razor, deodorant
    aspirin, prescriptions, Tampax
    face cream, powder, baby oil

TO CARRY:
mohair throw
typewriter
2 legal pads and pens
files
house key

This is a list which was taped inside my closet door in Hollywood during those years when I was reporting more or less steadily. The list enabled me to pack, without thinking, for any piece I was likely to do. Notice the deliberate anonymity of costume: in a skirt, a leotard, and stockings, I could pass on either side of the culture. Notice the mohair throw for trunk-line flights (i.e., no blankets) and for the motel room in which the air conditioning could not be turned off. Notice the bourbon for the same motel room. Notice the typewriter for the airport, coming home: the idea was to turn in the Hertz car, check in, find an empty bench, and start typing the day's notes.

It should be clear that this was a list made by someone who prized control, yearned after momentum, someone determined to play her role as if she had the script, heard her cues, knew the narrative. There is on this list one significant omission, one article I needed and never had: a watch. I needed a watch not during the day, when I could turn on the car radio or ask someone, but at night, in the motel. Quite often I would ask the desk for the time every half hour or so, until finally, embarrassed to ask again, I would call Los Angeles and ask my husband. In other words I had skirts, jerseys, leotards, pullover sweater, shoes, stockings, bra, nightgown, robe, slippers, cigarettes, bourbon, shampoo, toothbrush and paste, Basis soap, razor, deodorant, aspirin, prescriptions, Tampax, face cream, powder, baby oil, mohair throw, typewriter, legal pads, pens, files and a house key, but I didn't know what time it was. This may be a parable, either of my life as a reporter during this period or of the period itself.

Joan Didion

From the story "The Things They Carried"

The things they carried were largely determined by necessity. Among the necessities or near necessities were P-38 can openers, pocket knives, heat tabs, wrist watches, dog tags, mosquito repellent, chewing gum, candy, salt tablets, packets of Kool Aid, lighters, matches, sewing kits, Military Payment Certificates, C rations, and two or three canteens of water. . . . On their feet they carried jungle boots—2.1 pounds—and Dave Jensen carried three pairs of socks and a can of Dr. Scholl's foot powder as a precaution against trench foot. Until he was shot, Ted Lavender carried six or seven ounces of premium dope, which for him was a necessity. Mitchell Sanders, the RTO2, carried condoms. Norman Bowker carried a diary. Rat Kiley carried comic books. Kiowa, a devout Baptist, carried an illustrated New Testament that had been presented to him by his father, who taught Sunday school in Oklahoma City, Oklahoma. As a hedge against bad times, however, Kiowa also carried his grandmother's distrust of the white man, his grandfather's old hunting hatchet. Necessity dictated.

Tim O'Brien

At the Dinner Table

ociologists lament the fact that few of us sit down with our families each night to eat dinner together anymore. Instead, we catch the end of the evening news on television or chat on the phone with a friend while stuffing down a slice of cold pizza. While modern life may seem overly hectic and leave us longing for lost traditions, in truth many of us are privately relieved to give up the daily ritual of the family meal.

Family meals are inherently emotionally charged, even in the most reserved families. Stepsisters, who were fighting over the phone only minutes before, are forced to sit next to each other and pass the peas. Working parents hurry and try to catch up on their children's days even as their children are rolling their eyes and asking to be excused. Often our expectations—whether we long for harmony, serious conversation, or simply a feeling of togetherness—are dashed as the meatloaf dries out on the counter and the second glass of milk spills and fans out across the table. Still, it is there amid the chaos, disappointments, and second helpings of three-alarm chili that many of our memories remain.

Panning Instructions

1. Think back to your childhood dinner, lunch, or breakfast table. (Some of us will have to think back further than others.) Even if you ate only one or two meals a week (or month) as a family, focus on those meals. **Freewrite** for ten minutes on your family meals. If you find yourself getting stuck, prompt yourself by focusing on the smells and tastes of the foods you ate together.

2. Draw a simple sketch of your family's table. Was it round? square? oblong? Where did everyone sit? Draw pictures of your family members (you don't have to be an artist; stick figures will do) and seat them in their appropriate places at the table. Note the conflicts that existed between family members by writing applicable notes near the drawing that represents them (for example, "Mary resents Tony because he was the first to take her place as the only child—will never sit next to him").

3. What were some of the typical meals you ate? **List** several as you remember them and briefly note your reactions to them, as in the list below:

MEAL	REACTION
Macaroni and cheese	Felt loved when my mother remembered to sprinkle bread crumbs on top the way I liked.
TV dinners	Fought with my brother over who got the one that had the brownie for dessert.
Bacon and eggs	My father cooked these on Sundays sometimes before the divorce.

4. Begin a poem, short story, or personal essay in which you bring to life a particular meal at your childhood table. Choose a meal that is both ordinary and memorable. Perhaps an announcement of some kind was made (maybe someone was fired from a job, made cheerleading squad, was expelled from school, had joined a convent, or was moving to Mexico) or a family member had either joined the table (through birth, adoption, remarriage, and so on) or left (through divorce, death, high school graduation, and so forth).

Comb through your prewriting and choose the most telling concrete details—those that appeal to our sense of smell, taste, touch, hearing, and sight. If you're writing a poem or story, feel free to create characters and events. Try to incorporate stressful interactions that might have taken place. In the excerpt from the novel *Dinner at the Homesick Restaurant* (page 43), notice the tension between the three children and their mother, Pearl, soon after Pearl's husband has left them. In the short story "A Family Supper" (page 44), notice that much of the tension exists in what is left unsaid. And in the excerpt from Madelyn Callahan (page 43), notice that the dinner table serves as a unifying context for describing characters and their relationships.

Excavating Instructions

Take a step away from the table and try looking at yourself from the perspective of another family member. Write a piece in which a sibling, parent, or other relative tells a dinner table story that focuses on your behavior and features a major event in your life.

Or bring together in a story, essay, or poem both past and present controversial figures from your life (enemies, old bosses, teachers, and so on). Consider also including a few celebrities (Kevin Costner, for example). At this spectacularly odd dinner, introduce one topic for everyone to discuss and record the imaginary dialogue and interactions.

NUGGETS

From the essay "At the Dinner Table"

My father sat at the head of a large rectangular table, which overwhelmed the living and dining space in our Rob-and-Laura-Petrie-style home. At the other end of the table, my maternal grandmother made her nightly disapprovals clear with her stony silences and her expressionless mouth. To my father's right, my mother juggled dishes and serving utensils furiously, because, as I recall, the woman was consistently furious day and night. Between my parents was wedged the small, fat protoplasm with lungs that became my brother. . . .

I always sat at my father's left, torturing my older sister who was perfect. Perfectly neat. Perfectly attired. Perfectly coifed. Far more savvy than even Madonna, she created a myth of her own perfection at the age of seven.

MADELYN CALLAHAN

ARTIFACTS

From the novel *Dinner at the Homesick Restaurant*

The sounds from the kitchen were different now—cutlery rattling, glassware clinking. Their mother must be setting the table. Pretty soon she'd serve supper. Cody had such a loaded feeling in his throat, he never wanted to eat again. . . .

They filed down, dragging their feet. They stopped at the first-floor bathroom and meticulously scrubbed their hands, taking extra pains with the backs. Each one waited for the others. Then they went into the kitchen. Their mother was slicing a brick of Spam. She didn't look at them, but she started speaking the instant they were seated. "It's not enough that I should have to work till 5:00 P.M., no; then I come home and find nothing seen to, no chores done, you children off till all hours with disreputable characters in the alleys or wasting your time with school chorus, club meetings. . . ."

She sat serenely, as if finished with the subject forever, and reached for a bowl of peas. Jenny's face was streaming with tears, but she wasn't making a sound and Pearl seemed unaware of her. Cody cleared his throat. . . .

The three of them washed the dishes, dried them, and put them away in the cupboards. They wiped the table and countertops and swept the kitchen floor. The sight of any crumb or stain was a relief, a pleasure; they attacked it with Bon Ami.

ANNE TYLER

From the short story "A Family Supper"

Supper was waiting in a dimly lit room next to the kitchen. The only source of light was a big lantern that hung over the table, casting the rest of the room in shadow. We bowed to each other before starting the meal.

There was little conversation. When I made some polite comment about the food, Kikuko giggled a little. Her earlier nervousness seemed to have returned to her. My father did not speak for several minutes. Finally he said:

"It must feel strange for you, being back in Japan."

"Yes, it is a little strange."

"Already, perhaps, you regret leaving America."

"A little. Not so much. I didn't leave behind much. Just some empty rooms."

"I see."

I glanced across the table. My father's face looked stony and forbidding in the half-light. We ate on in silence.

KAZUO ISHIGURO

Paper Trails

Those who have gone through the agony of an IRS audit know the value of canceled checks and credit-card receipts as records of possible deductible expenses. But canceled checks and other historical documents, such as old school papers, calling cards, and invoices, are more than that. Pull out a stack of canceled checks or credit-card statements from several years ago and fan through them. Notice how your life, or your spending, has changed over the years. Mixed in with the routine checks you will also find one-time payments that often reflect significant events during certain periods of your life, the $5 check paid to the county for a marriage license (remember your consternation at not having cash and the thought that a license to marry someone could cost so little); the $1,700 you paid out-of-pocket for necessary dental work (at the time, and even now, an extraordinary amount of money); the $30 check for an office visit to the doctor and an examination that confirmed a pregnancy.

Other documents can also spark memories and feelings. A yellowed sixth-grade history test can send you into a pit of poignancy—you said the capital of Washington state was Washington, D.C., and your teacher wrote "Nice try."

The following exercises ask you to exploit the imaginative potential in seemingly inconsequential historical documents that remain tucked in purses and backpacks and stacked and rubber-banded in storage.

Panning Instructions

1. Look over a group of canceled checks and credit-card statements and make a list of items for which you paid about the same amount of money. For example, you may have written three checks for $25 each—one check to a babysitter, another to purchase a camping lantern, and another for a pair of jeans. In a story, poem, or essay, try to connect several checks written for a similar amount.

2. Gather several old discarded documents, such as invoices, report cards, doctor bills, or ATM receipts, and construct a story, poem, or essay around them. The documents may be integral to the plot or theme of what you are writing, or they may simply appear in your story, poem, or essay.

☀️ Excavating Instructions

1. From your collection of canceled checks and credit-card statements, choose five or six purchases made around the same time that evoke strong feelings or memories or that seem particularly revealing. Notice how humorist Art Buchwald, in "Credit Card" (see page 47), uses the occasion of the theft of one of his credit cards to reveal his tastes. Begin a poem, story, or essay about what was going on in your life when these checks were written or charge receipts were signed. The piece should integrate the information on all the checks and receipts. For example, the student poem "The Giraffe" (see below) uses the following information from checks the student wrote in 1979:

#506, July 16, Toys "R" Us	$ 178.00
#507, July 19, John Elman, Atty.	$3,290.00
#508, August 10, IRS	$2,140.19
#509, August 12, Towson Funeral Services	$7,200.00

2. Or from both canceled checks and credit-card statements, take note of those expenses that arose in an emergency of some sort, and use these incidents in a poem, story, or essay.

👹 NUGGETS

The Giraffe
I bought a giraffe the size of a house
for my grandson just before my wife died.
It wasn't an easy time, but the giraffe
struck me funny, so much so
that when the IRS and my attorney
came knocking, I let them in
to my savings. What matter? My grandson
doesn't know what to do with the giraffe,
but he shows it off and his friends come over
and they all stare up at it. I've never seen a toy
that big. I've never seen anything
that big.

ARNOLD PETROWSKI

 **ARTIFACTS**

From the column "Credit Card"

Recently one of my credit cards was stolen. The problem was that I was unaware of the theft, and therefore the criminal had use of the card for thirty days. . . .

"Did you have fun in Puerto Rico?" my accountant wanted to know.

"Not really," I told him. "Mainly because I haven't been there in ten years."

"Well, you got a credit card bill for three thousand dollars for a stay there, and it looks as if you had a wonderful shopping spree. I wish you would tell your wife to buy quarts instead of gallons of Joy perfume."

"That wasn't my wife," I protested. "She hates Joy. It's obvious that some-one else is using my card. . . ."

"You don't have to pay the charges once you report the loss," he assured me.

"I'm not worried about that. I'm concerned he's going to hurt my reputa-tion as a big spender. Suppose he buys his socks at People's Drug Store? . . ."

". . . Your friend bought a beautiful cashmere jacket at Barney's for fourteen hundred dollars."

"Single- or double-breasted?"

"Single."

"That's good," I said. "I hate double-breasted."

ART BUCHWALD

i Have Been Eating Boredom

Boredom is that condition or state that results when will and imagination go on vacation together leaving us with nothing but time. Most of us have suffered this condition at one time or another, most typically during adolescence, but boredom can descend at any other time or age. While those suffering from boredom sometimes are accused of being lazy, some psychologists believe that boredom is almost the opposite of laziness. They assert that boredom is the expression or manifestation of too many ideas and desires tugging in opposite directions. One psychologist said boredom was rather like an airplane at full take-off throttle with its brakes on: an extraordinary amount of energy is being expended both to move the plane and to prevent it from moving.

Whatever the truth about boredom, there is little question that most of us dread it. The following exercise is intended not necessarily to cure boredom but to use boredom as a creative resource.

Panning Instructions

1. Since boredom often is such an inclusive state, it invites desperate ideas and imagery and considerable poetic license. Complete the following prompts with the part of speech indicated and continue elaborating until you have material to begin a poem, story, or essay:

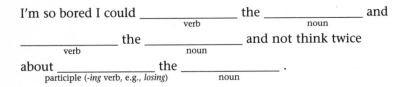

I'm so bored I could _____ the _____ and
                                verb   noun

_____ the _____ and not think twice
   verb   noun

about _____ the _____ .
   participle (-*ing* verb, e.g., *losing*)   noun

2. Replace a major character or concept in a famous story or poem with the word *boredom* and endow this character or concept with your sense or vision of boredom. For example, you might replace Edgar Allan Poe's Raven with boredom, or create a bored Cinderella or Moby Dick. Mark Strand's famous poem in celebration of poetry begins with "I have been eating / poetry / there is no happiness / like mine." You might write "I have been eating boredom / there is no hollowness like mine." Alternatively, you could replace concepts or characters from several stories or poems with boredom and string them all together.

Excavating Instructions

Remember a time when you were so bored you couldn't move, or imagine a character in this state. Quite often in such a position, we consider dozens of ideas for things to do but, owing to boredom's very nature, we reject them all in favor of stasis, often with very elaborate and ingenious reasons and rationalizations for why we can't do them. In this exercise, list a few ideas for relieving boredom; for each one, develop reasons why you or the character you have created simply can't carry them out. For example:

> He considered going to the library to get the book he had ordered, but the problem was it was probably hot out and he doubted that he had a quarter for parking. Also, he might run into Professor Knight and have to explain his absence from class. He also didn't particularly like the smell of the library or the sense that it gave him that he was worthless . . . so the library was out.

Use the result as the beginning or premise of a story, poem, or essay.

NUGGETS

This Not Knowing What to Do
this not knowing what to do
did nothing that was not bad
it sat in a corner by a pan
and waited for something to call its name

not knowing what to do
slept with not knowing what to want
but nothing happened that was bad

and yet not knowing what to do
was encouraged by nothing that went wrong
who said that it was okay
to wait for anything to call its name

CARMEN DELGADO

 **ARTIFACTS**

Dream Song 14

Life, friends, is boring. We must not say so.
After all, the sky flashes, the great sea yearns,
we ourselves flash and yearn,
and moreover my mother told me as a boy
(repeatingly) "Ever to confess you're bored
means you have no

Inner Resources." I conclude now I have no
inner resources, because I am heavy bored.
Peoples bore me,
literature bores me, especially great literature,
Henry bores me, with his plight & gripes
as bad as achilles,

who loves people and valiant art, which bores me.
And the tranquil hills, & gin, look like a drag
and somehow a dog
has taken itself & its tail considerably away
into mountains or sea or sky, leaving
behind: me, wag.

                                        JOHN BERRYMAN

Home Contractors

Whether we own our own home, rent an apartment, live in a dorm, or even sublet a houseboat, when rain pours into the bedroom, a toilet refuses to stop flushing, or a pilot light continually blows out, we're forced to open our doors to virtual strangers, supposed experts in their fields. If we're lucky, these folks come recommended to us, but more often than not, in our desperation, we grab their names out of the Yellow Pages, our spirits temporarily buoyed by splashy advertisements that promise "24-Hour Expert Service," "Family-Owned Business," or "37 Years of Experience."

We skip work, class, a lunch date we planned a week before and wait—sometimes for hours—for these modern-day knights in shining armor to arrive. They use our telephones, our bathrooms. We offer them coffee, a soda, lead them to the crisis area and stand around feeling suddenly strange in our own homes, while they diagnose our problem and tell us what it will cost to repair.

Often, complications occur. Instead of a leak in a roof being repaired, a new one is created. Replaced tiles are two shades lighter, and looking at them makes you feel dizzy every time you step out of the bathtub. Work contracted for is never quite completed; tools are left behind. Strangers have been let into your life.

While these transactions can go smoothly, it is the unexpected developments that stay with us long after our toilets are flushing normally again. In these exercises, you will explore the creative possibilities home contractors provide us.

Panning Instructions

1. Think back and make a **list** of as many of the home contractors—including carpet cleaners, cabinet makers, architects, closet organizers, or repair folks—you can remember letting into your or your parents' home. Next to each entry, jot down a brief description of the situation and person, as in the following examples:

- Guy who redid our kitchen—those shiny white cabinet doors—red clipboard, pencil behind his ear
- Plumber who pulled all that hair out of the shower drain—lectured me about my long hair

2. Review your list and circle the three encounters that you remember as being the most problematic, for whatever reason.

3. Begin a poem, story, or essay in which this encounter figures prominently. As you write, feel free to fictionalize any aspects of the encounter for effect.

Excavating Instructions

Sometimes the things that need fixing in our homes are much less tangible than a leaky faucet or a clogged drainpipe. We take out second mortgages to add on a family room when our family is, in fact, dissolving around us. We pay someone to tune a piano that we never get around to learning how to play. We have a burglar alarm installed to keep strangers out when we are feeling acutely alone.

Continue with your current beginning of a story, poem, or essay and allude indirectly to its deeper significance, or choose another encounter from your list and begin a new story, poem, or essay that does this.

NUGGETS

From a creative essay

For ten years, the brown carpet of my tiny house was regularly cleaned by George's Carpet Care. Paul, George's loyal employee for the last 15 years, usually did most of the work. He moved the couch, tables, beds, and hoisted the heavy, steaming hose around the rooms in a logically thorough pattern.

Three months ago my family and I moved to a new home. The carpet was in need of a good cleaning and I called George's Carpet Care. I warned Paul to keep the water end of the hose away from our new piano, and then showed him the rest of the house. I could smell his two-pack-a-day habit following us down the hall. After he measured all the rooms and gave me my estimate, he and George unloaded the truck and started up the equipment.

George started cleaning the bedroom and after awhile, Paul took over pushing and pulling the stainless steel hose around. When Paul got to the living room he passed the hose to George. Paul sat down at the piano and began playing a lovely piece. I was stunned by his talent but over-protective of the piano. I asked Paul, "Are your hands clean?" He got up instantly and didn't sit down again.

DEBBY THOMPSON

 **ARTIFACTS**

From the short story "The Least You Need to Know"

"Let me tell you, Mr. Silver. It's not easy what I do." My father reached into his coveralls and pulled out a piece of white enamel the length and shape of one of my mother's nail files. "Do you know what this is?" Leon Silver shook his head. "We call it a bone in the business. It's what I use to scrape up blood stains. I wet the stain with spotter and then I get down on my knees and start scraping. The blood foams up, and let me tell you, you don't forget the smell of blood—rotten—it stays with you." He tossed the bone toward the coffee table, and it landed on the crown of Leon Silver's fedora. "That's what I was doing when this girl's mother sat down on the floor beside me to watch." I felt Leon Silver press his shoulders into the back of the sofa. "Why would she want to do that, Mr. Silver? Can you answer me that?"

"No," said Leon Silver. "I don't know anything about that."

"That's right," said my father. "You don't know. But me, I'm there trying to do my job. It's a job someone has to do, right?"

LEE MARTIN

Honey, I'm Home

Who among us hasn't come home early to find things not exactly as we had imagined? Perhaps your roommate is sitting in his underpants on the couch and clipping his toenails. Maybe your children have been left in front of a blaring television while the babysitter chats on the phone to her boyfriend. Even when we live alone we can be surprised. Recently, a story about a landlord caught on videotape doing all sorts of odd things, including rearranging the food in his tenant's refrigerator—and worse—was heavily publicized in the media.

We expect life to function in our homes in a reasonable, logical manner in our absence. When we come home early from school or work or even running errands and find something amiss, we can feel baffled, unmoored. Home is supposed to be a place in which, kings and queens or princes and princesses of our domains, we rule—or at least know what to expect.

While most of us prefer to avoid domestic surprises in our ongoing lives, they can serve as inspiration for writing, as in the following exercises.

Panning Instructions

1. Begin by **listing** all the times you have either taken someone you live with by surprise or have yourself been taken by surprise by a change in a normal daily schedule. If you live alone now, think back to a time when you lived with someone else, perhaps as a child in your family. The following are examples:

- Time I came home in the middle of the day and caught Vikki watching that soap
- When John had trouble explaining those green socks
- Time that my mom smelled smoke in my bedroom

Choose the one that caused you the most anxiety and try **clustering** around it. Remember, when you cluster one bubble leads into another in any way that strikes you at the moment.

2. Using your cluster as raw material, begin a story, poem, or essay that further explores this event.

Excavating Instructions

Sometimes people get caught when they're so full of guilt they're actually glad to get caught, or we catch someone doing something that we already suspected he or she was hiding. The moments around these domestic encounters are still intense, though. In fact, they're often more so because they confirm our, or a loved one's, worst suspicions.

Going back to your original list with this idea in mind, begin a story, poem, or essay that examines one of these complex moments of discovery. Be sure to include dialog in this beginning. Remember that people usually talk *around* issues when they have something to hide.

NUGGETS

Honey, I'm Home
(for Se)

Walked in on you sleeping
rather angelic
for someone as cursed as you
walked back out
and knocked
wanted to pretend to
have never seen the sight of you
twirled up in those sheets
black masses of hair enveloping you
I found you beautiful
like a nymph
but I, with no words to say
frowned, remembered
the echoes of my footsteps
as I walked away

KELENE STEVENS

ARTIFACTS

From the short story "Preservation"

Late one afternoon she came home from work, parked the car, and went inside the house. She could hear the TV going in the living room as she let herself in the door to the kitchen. The coffee pot was on the stove, and the burner was on low. From where she stood in the kitchen, holding her purse, she could look into the living room and see the back of the sofa and the TV screen. Figures moved across the screen. Her husband's bare feet stuck out from one end of the sofa. At the other end, on a pillow which lay across the arm of the sofa, she could see the crown of his head. He didn't stir. He may or may not have been asleep, and he may or may not have heard her come in. But she decided it didn't make any difference one way or other. She put her purse on the table and went over to the fridge to get herself some yogurt. But when she opened the door, warm, boxed-in air came out at her. She couldn't believe the mess inside. The ice cream from the freezer had melted and run down into the leftover fish sticks and cole slaw. Ice cream had gotten into the bowl of Spanish rice and pooled on the bottom of the fridge. Ice cream was everywhere. She opened the door to the freezer compartment. An awful smell puffed out at her that made her want to gag. Ice cream covered the bottom of the compartment and puddled around a three-pound package of hamburger. She pressed her finger into the cellophane wrapper covering the meat, and her finger sank into the package. The pork chops had thawed, too. Everything had thawed, including some more fish sticks, a package of Steak-ums, and two Chef Sammy Chinese food dinners. The hot dogs and homemade spaghetti sauce had thawed. She closed the door to the freezer and reached into the fridge for her carton of yogurt. She raised the lid of the yogurt and sniffed. That's when she yelled at her husband.

RAYMOND CARVER

The Evolution of Mini-Skills

Ordinarily we think of the word "skills" as applying to fairly substantial chunks of useful behavior. Common skills include the ability to write, to type, to drive a car, to operate a computer, to speak Spanish.

However, there are other behaviors that might qualify as skills, but, because they don't seem particularly useful, we never get credit for possessing them. Notice how a child develops proficiency crawling backward or taking a block from one bucket and putting it in another.

As adults we become expert at knowing exactly how much flour equals a cup without having to measure, at jiggling the toilet handle, just so, to keep the water from running, at carrying on a phone conversation while putting away groceries and balancing a checkbook. Though perhaps minor on some scale, these are skills, nevertheless, and we should get credit for them and celebrate our competence.

Panning Instructions

1. Pay close attention to your domestic behavior and the behaviors of others you may live with, and make a note of any little thing that might qualify as an unlikely and unacknowledged skill. Make a **list** of such skills.

2. Choose one or more of these skills to examine more fully in a poem, short story, or essay. Be sure to give the development of this skill respect. You may even want to give it an "epic" flavor as Bill Watkins does in "Rolling the Clothes Dryer Lint into a Ball" (page 58).

Excavating Instructions

For an even greater challenge, think of an emotional skill you have mastered, such as denial, looking on the bright side, and so on, and write a poem, story, or essay that explores the meaning, origin, or manifestation of this skill. For an example of this challenge, notice the way Mona Simpson's character has mastered the skill of sleeping (page 58) or how the narrator of Elizabeth Bishop's poem "One Art" has conquered losing (page 59). In the brief excerpt from their essay "On Quitting," Shelly Ross and Evan Harris dignify what, for most of us, would be a failure (see page 59).

 # NUGGETS

Rolling the Clothes Dryer Lint into a Ball
How long I had thrown this lint away
Fabric of my care-worn days
Without stopping once to feel and shape
the remnants of this piebald waste

BILL WATKINS

Vid Kid
My grandson Nintendo plays
His fingers move faster than tiddly-winks
Which, by the way, he can't play
When it comes to dialing my phone
Again, he can't—it's not touch tone

LORRAINE SMITS

From the essay "Zippo"
I remember that as a young boy I could light a cigarette in the wind and the other boys in the neighborhood could not. So it followed that I would light a cigarette in the wind whenever I could.

I told my friends, "The secret lies in the magic of the Zippo." Talented youngster that I was, I whipped out the Zippo so fast that the centrifugal force alone flipped open the lid . . . against gale force winds my cupped hands kept the flame alive . . . this was my talent.

SEAN CARTER

ARTIFACTS

From the novel *The Lost Father*
I slept, and could sleep, anywhere. Under a sheet, my limbs would move in the thick pleasure of being unseen. I could sleep most times, especially if I had something warm. I dressed in layers of cotton and would leave some piece, a sweatshirt or a T-shirt, on top of a radiator. Then I took the warm thing and hugged it in my arms by my face and before the heat drained out of it I was fast asleep. I did that in boys' apartments to help assuage the strangeness. I always woke up first in the morning.

MONA SIMPSON

One Art

The art of losing isn't hard to master;
so many things seem filled with the intent
to be lost that their loss is no disaster.

Lose something every day. Accept the fluster
of lost door keys, the hour badly spent.
The art of losing isn't hard to master.

Then practice losing farther, losing faster:
places, and names, and where it was you meant
to travel. None of these will bring disaster.

I lost my mother's watch. And look! My last, or
next-to-last, of three loved houses went.
The art of losing isn't hard to master.

I lost two cities, lovely ones. And, vaster,
some realms I owned, two rivers, a continent.
I miss them, but it wasn't a disaster.

Even losing you (the joking voice, a gesture
I love) I shan't have lied. It's evident
the art of losing's not too hard to master
though it may look like (Write it!) like disaster.

ELIZABETH BISHOP

From the essay "On Quitting"

First, the quitter thinks about quitting. This stage includes contemplating unhappiness, frustration, and shame, and dwelling on discomforts, injustices, and boredom. It can satisfy the quitter for months or even years. Next the quitter fantasizes about methods of quitting. This is often the most creative part of the process, and many quitters draw it out, letting the imaginative quality that is inherent in many quitters come to the fore. Finally, the quitter quits.

SHELLY ROSS AND EVAN HARRIS

The Note Read, "There Are More Where These Came From"

In many homes, as roommates, spouses, children, and parents prepare to head out the door in the morning, they quickly fill each other in on the day's upcoming events while buttering their toast. Some days we may catch up by phone; other days we may find ourselves scribbling brief notes to remind a son to start dinner, a wife that we have a seven o'clock meeting, a roommate that it's her turn to take the recycling bin to the curb. If we live alone, we may write notes to ourselves to remind us of deadlines, appointments, and phone calls we need to return.

At the time they are written, these short notes usually succeed at communicating their points, but even just days later their content can seem cryptic, obscure, and baffling. The abbreviated language can also serve as creative inspiration, as in the following exercise.

Panning Instructions

1. Write several different short notes that you might actually leave for a person you live with or for yourself if you live alone. The notes should fit into the following categories:

- **Informational** ("I'll be home late tonight"; "Help!—We're out of milk"; "I'm taping so don't turn off the VCR"; "Remember to call Jack.")
- **Emotional** ("I'm sorry I yelled this morning"; "I love you anyway"; "Let's celebrate later.")
- **Absurd** ("The cat ate the gerbil"; "I invented Pig Latin"; "You will never win at Scrabble"; "I saw a unicorn on the Beltway this morning.")

2. Using one of these notes as a starting point, begin a poem, story, or essay that challenges our initial expectations. What does your note tell us about you? about the person you wrote it to? about the life you are living? Or write a piece in which you combine several of the notes in an imaginative way, as Alex McNeal does below in his poem "Notes."

☀ Excavating Instructions

Use the short note form to tell someone you live with something honest and surprising about him or yourself—for example, "I have always hated the way you scramble eggs"; "I love your phony English accent"; "I'm tired of washing your dirty socks"; "You look handsome when you forget to shave"; "I want a pet monkey"; "I don't want to live with you anymore." If you live alone, astonish yourself with your revelation.

Try writing a poem in note form that explores this confession. Or work on a story or essay in which this note serves as a catalyst for further insights.

兀 NUGGETS

Notes

Went to movies. Be back
11ish. Pick up some Lysol. Bathroom. Ugh!!!
Saw your old girl friend. Ugh!!!
We're out of beer man. How come?
Every lightbulb in this house
is out. Cool, uh?
Saw your ex again. Mind
if I call her? (Kidding.)
Why six jars of sauerkraut? Were they on sale
or have you gone funny?
I aced the psych test but I'm still
depressed.
Saw your ex again. She asked about you. Can you believe she's a Road
     Test Dummies freak?
Your mom called. No message. Sounded happy, as usual.
Your mom called again. Guess you didn't get back.
Something about your dad. Better call.
Saw Kim again. She got a tattoo on her inner thigh. How come I know
     that?
One lightbulb?? Eight rooms? Cool.

ALEX McNEAL

 ## ARTIFACTS

From the short story "Nothing to Do with Love"

I would call this all a dream, but the note she left perched for me on the nightstand beside my bed was real. I gave it to the officer at the Bureau of Missing Persons. He took it in his hand and acknowledged its substance.

Mom,
    I don't expect you to understand. This has nothing to do with love, but I'm leaving. I just had to get out of this house. Sometime soon I'll get in touch.

Robin

She is right: I do not understand. But she is wrong: this has everything to do with love.

Joyce Reiser Kornblatt

Quilting

Even those of us who claim not to be materialistic can't help but form attachments to certain clothes. Like fragments from old songs, clothes can evoke both cherished and painful memories. A worn-thin, gauzy dress may hang in the back of a closet even though it hasn't been worn in years because the faint scent of pine that lingers on it is all that remains of someone's sixteenth summer. An impractical white muff might be pulled out of a donation bag at the last minute because of the promise of elegance it once held for its owner. And a ripped T-shirt might be rescued from the dustrag bin long after the name of the band once emblazoned across it has faded into oblivion.

Clothes document personal history for writers in the same way that fossils chart time for archaeologists. In these exercises, you will dig through your closets and drawers to explore the creative possibilities for writing that clothing can uncover.

Panning Instructions

1. Root through your closet and drawers and locate clothing that was significant to you during different times in your life. (Even those who are "good" about getting rid of old clothes should find enough recent memories to complete this exercise.) Create a **list** of the clothes that have special meaning for you.

2. Label the event(s) that each item on your list of clothing causes you to recall, as well as the feelings it evoked, as in the list below.

Clothing	Event	Feeling
Angora sweater	ice-skating party	lonely, Brian didn't show up
White bathrobe	quiet nights in my first apartment	peaceful, independent
Blue suit	job interviews	nervous, young, overprepared

3. Begin a poem, story, or essay based on one or more of these items of clothing. To discover the connections that exist between the items, try dedicating a stanza or paragraph to each item and letting the relationships between the pieces unfold naturally.

If you decide to work on a poem, try creating your own quilt pattern by using the same number of lines in each stanza and beginning each stanza with the same words or structures, as in the student poem "Don't Ask Me" (see below).

Excavating Instructions

Add to your quilt by including scraps of clothing that belong to someone who is close to you or who was once close to you. If the clothing actually exists in closets and drawers that are accessible, you may want to begin by selecting several pieces and labeling them as you did above. It's more likely, however, that this clothing has been stored exclusively in your mind's eye. If that's the case, sort through your memory and see what important fragments remain. Notice the power a blue jacket takes on in the poem "How It Is" by Maxine Kumin (see page 66).

NUGGETS

Don't Ask Me
Don't ask me about the red.
The hem of the bright red orlon sweater
given me one Christmas
became hopelessly caught in a carnivorous
zipper and appalled my lovely third grade teacher.

Don't ask me about the white.
The collar of my best white shirt
should have had lipstick on it
but remained as virginal as a priest
who was really a saint.

ROBERT METTLER

World Quilt
beige corduroy square of Somalia
cloth dry as the trees stripped

of leaves, stripped of bark boiled
into thin stringy soup, where hope
is diarrhea eating away the flesh
of children. O, rumpled land

worn down to the nap . . .

Lorraine Smits

From *An Idea So Foreign,* a novel in progress

Sometimes Elaine tried on clothes late at night while the radio voices prattled away. She had gone back to work when Terry was sixteen months old, and over the years had amassed a substantial wardrobe. Expert at buying expensive clothes at discount prices—she could recognize a name brand even with three-fourths of a label cut out—Elaine had accumulated an impressive collection of linen suits, A-line skirts, wool slacks and silk blouses. While the cuts and fabrics of her clothes were conservative, she favored bright, even dramatic, colors that had made her pale skin gleam when she was younger. But the lemon yellows, lime greens and sugar-plum pinks that had once made her feel brisk and efficient as she clicked in her two-inch heels down the hallway of the office where she worked, now made her skin appear sallow and seemed to deepen the pockets under her eyes and darken the splotches that stained her hands and forearms.

Suzanne Greenberg

ARTIFACTS

From the poem "Ode to My Socks"
Maru Mori brought me
a pair
of socks
which she knitted herself
with her sheep-herder's hands,
two socks as soft
as rabbits.
I slipped my feet
into them as though into
two
cases knitted
with threads of
twilight . . .

Pablo Neruda

From the poem "How It Is"

Shall I say how it is in your clothes?
A month after your death I wear your blue jacket.
The dog at the center of my life recognizes
you've come to visit, he's ecstatic.
In the left pocket, a hole.
In the right, a parking ticket
delivered up last August on Bay State Road.
In my heart, a scatter like milkweed,
a flinging from the pods of my soul.
My skin presses your old outline.
It is hot and dry inside . . .

MAXINE KUMIN

The Family Normal

To hear their stories, you would think that all families have black sheep, those maligned souls who fell short of or deviated from a family's cherished values or aims: the daughter who preferred tending bar to tending children, the son who broke the long line of lawyers and decided to join the Peace Corps, the nephew who loves working at the 7-Eleven, despite his Ph.D.

Often, though, the supposed rebel is in fact taking her cues from the family's unspoken values. For example, the daughter who has been shunned by her family after being fired for suspected embezzlement learned how to defraud by watching her father do his taxes. And the student who drops out of college to take care of his sick grandmother after his parents worked long hours at jobs they didn't like so he could have an education is only exemplifying what they have shown him they value: sacrifice.

In the following exercises you will examine your family's not-so-obvious values and explore the creative potential of hidden traditions.

Panning Instructions

1. For this assignment, try to discover your family's values by filling in the blanks after the following prompts:

- The event/relative my family never talks about is _____ .
- The only thing my parents ever lied about was _____ .
- If families could create holidays, ours would be to celebrate the day that _____ .
- In my family, the worst thing that could happen to you is _____ .
- If my family had its own coat of arms, the colors would be _____ , _____ , _____ , and the animal would be a _____ .

2. Look over your responses and **freewrite** or **free associate** on some of the values—patriotism, thrift, honesty, education—your family held (either the family you belonged to growing up or the family you have since created on your own). Be sure to focus not only on the values they claim as values, but also those implied by gestures and behaviors. For example, several people in a family may have filed bankruptcy. Though no one specifically advocated this measure, filing bankruptcy became an expectation for you as an adult.

Focus on a questionable expectation or value and begin a poem, story, or essay showing how it created conflict for an individual who "fell short."

Excavating Instructions

Start a poem, story, or essay that spotlights one specific occasion when one of your family's values was taken to a ludicrous or extreme level. For example, maybe your family cherishes getting a "good deal" so much that your mother and you spent months searching for your prom dress at yard sales before breaking down and going to a department store. Or maybe your family values competition so much that your children spent an entire week at the beach indoors staging a Monopoly tournament. If you're working on a poem or story, feel free to exaggerate the facts for effect.

In your writing, consider some of the reasons for the value being taken to this extreme, as well as the toll it might be taking on various members of the family. For instance, perhaps children who are playing Monopoly all week at the beach feel safer competing among each other than they do interacting with strangers they might meet. Ultimately, isolation and loneliness might be some of the effects of this value being taken so far. In the following excerpt from "Beauty Shop," notice the way Joanne Bogazzi begins to examine how worrying over their hair hides other problems that her mother and she might be sharing.

NUGGETS

From "Beauty Shop," an essay in progress

This was the fourth beauty shop we had visited this month, and the smell of hairspray, cigarette smoke and well-thumbed-through magazines almost seemed like home to me. I saw my mother every Saturday afternoon when I picked her up from the nursing home for our weekly visit. It didn't matter that each time I came with a different plan for the afternoon—from visiting a museum to seeing a matinee to just plain going somewhere to talk—we always ended up doing the same thing, trying to find the one beautician in all of Atlanta who could meet my mother's exacting qualifications.

Hair was an obsession with her, and try as I might not to, I had inherited this unfortunate family fixation. Not that you could tell to look at me. Much to my mother's horror, I wore my own hair short and straight as a little boy's, but secretly I was as obsessed as she was with the perfect hairstyle. I was just more savvy about hiding my fixation.

I wondered lately if our obsession with the perfect hair style hid a deeper obsession, a panic that I had, and perhaps she shared, about the rest of our clearly unfocused, unexacting lives, her short, failed marriages, my sense of seemingly permanent dislocation. Even as we paid fastidious attention to the exact proportions of her haircuts, of the relationship between bangs and forehead, highlights and layers, the rest of both of our lives seemed to be drifting past us. I wanted to talk to my mother about what was inside of her; instead we focused on the outside, on the frazzled, split, overprocessed strands of her remaining hair.

JOANNE BOGAZZI

The Family Normal

We had snakes in our garden
because we were that kind of family:
cousins would change gender, aunts
would disappear on singles' cruises
through the Bermuda Triangle.

My paternal grandfather pole-vaulted
for a hobby until he was seventy,
and his wife gleefully set fires
in other people's bathrooms.

Is it any wonder I'm without wife
and credit? Yes, a wonder
because my father
before going off to a monastery
in the shadow of the French Pyrenees
said I was to be "the family normal."
Watching me protect my friends
from my relatives, he knew
I held the one chromosome
untouched by the moon. And I knew,
the morning my mother walked naked
into the A&P, I'd keep this thing to myself.

But then, they were only garter snakes,
good long sad fellows.

MICHAEL JENKINS

 ARTIFACTS

From the short story "The Water-Faucet Vision"

To protect my sister Mona and me from the pains—or, as they pronounced it, the "pins"—of life, my parents did their fighting in Shanghai dialect, which we didn't understand; and when my father one day pitched a brass vase through the kitchen window, my mother told us he had done it by accident.

"By accident?" said Mona.

My mother chopped the foot off a mushroom.

"By accident?" said Mona. "By *accident?*"

Later I tried to explain to her that she shouldn't have persisted like that, but it was hopeless.

"What's the matter with throwing things," she shrugged. "He was mad."

GISH JEN

Photo Album

Most of us have good intentions when it comes to organizing photographs. We purchase thick albums and plan to begin sorting through that messy drawer or box as soon as we get a little free time. Meanwhile, last year's Christmas pictures are mingling with photographs from the year before, and it's virtually impossible to tell which Thanksgiving turkey Uncle Robert is proudly basting. Photographs of new babies all begin to resemble each other, and soon we may find ourselves arguing with another family member over whether that woman wearing the striking boa is a distant relative who showed up at Grandma and Grandpa's golden wedding anniversary or a costumed attorney who danced by herself all night at a Mardi Gras party a few years back.

This exercise will be of no help to you if your goal is simply to organize your photographs. Instead, the exercise is designed to help you disorganize them even more in hopes of making surprising new connections.

Panning Instructions

1. Choose two photographs of people you know but who have never met each other. They may be the same age but on two different sides of your family; they may both be ex-boyfriends or girlfriends; or they may exist in different times entirely (for example, your deceased great-grandmother and your two-year-old nephew). Beginning with their first names, **free associate** on each of the photos for five minutes. Don't be hemmed in by what you know about the people whose photos you have chosen. Instead, as with all free associations, allow the words you come up with to lead you to new discoveries.

2. Introduce these people to each other by clearing off a space on your desk or kitchen table and placing the photographs next to each other. Study the expressions on their faces. Is your father-in-law sneering at your childhood best friend, who smiles back at him, oblivious? Why is your second cousin twice removed batting her eyes at your next-door neighbor, who seems to be demonstrating how to bite off a hangnail? **Freewrite** on this new relationship for ten minutes.

3. Begin a poem or story in which these two characters meet. Use what you know about their personalities as you describe the encounter, as Selma Jackson does in "I Have Married My Father's Eyes" (below). Or, if you prefer, make up character traits to enhance your poem or story.

If you would rather work on a piece of creative nonfiction, explain why these two people should know each other, what they could add to each other's lives. You might try beginning with the line "It's too bad that _____ and _____ never met."

☼ Excavating Instructions

Insert yourself in your story, poem, or essay by exploring the reasons why you are bringing these two people together. What are your associations with each of them? Do they know different parts of you? Why would your life be better, more complete, if they knew each other?

🕺 NUGGETS

From the short story "I Have Married My Father's Eyes"

It's something I do every five or six years: go through and try to organize photographs into their chronological sequence. The problem is that lately I don't have a ghost of an idea as to when what happened, so the challenge is to approximate our personal history as best I can. Did Frank and I go to the Grand Canyon before or after my sister Mildred graduated from college? Were we descending the canyon walls on burros before Eddie took this picture of his daughter playing the role of Martha in *Who's Afraid of Virginia Woolf?* Had we already gazed upon the surreal oddness of the London Bridge in Lake Havasu City, Arizona, by the time that picture of Frank in his new snorkeling goggles was taken? Beats me. And here, what's this picture of my father doing right next to Frank's picture? Now there would be a meeting! If my father had been alive when I met and started going out with Frank, all hell would have been paid. And yet in some ways—in ways they would never acknowledge—they are alike. Dad rarely said anything twice; ditto for Frank. Hell, Frank rarely says anything once.

SELMA JACKSON

 **ARTIFACTS**

Brothers & Sisters
1

Even among your family you stand off to one side,
your big, dead face at last benign. The picture's
not dated, but everybody's poormouthed, pale, sun-
in-the-eye, the background data circa nineteen
sixty-nine. The photography functional. Your sisters look like
    part of the class, your
brothers part of the company. With some formality
each of you holds your own other hand. You're
practically the parent here, though it's Paul
who's about to complain to the camera: the angle's wrong,
too much sun. Everybody's blue or brown suit is shining.

2

We're out of the movies. The pictures don't lie,
Vivien Leigh is snow white Blanche DuBois. She has
a sister, the one everybody says you look like.
It is nineteen fifty-one, summer, and out on the sidewalk
the mere sun is blinding, tag-end. This is the matinee.
I saw you naked once, the lady at her bath. It's true,
you looked like somebody else. I had never seen so much
flesh. I ran the movie over and over. Pictures don't lie.
In the fifties photograph you still look like somebody's
brilliant sister, the girl in time, all face, too beautiful
but good, who's doting too completely on the boy.

3

In school we were told to draw our parents. Everybody
made moons—great pumpkin smiling moons, vegetable moons,
elliptical moons, moons like sad maps, eyes, ears, nose,
and chinless moons. We even cut black paper for cameos.
All of the faces floated in the dead air of pictures.
For years now their faces have run together. My father's
lives in my mother's as if by blood. Brother and sister.
She looks down at me from the dream as through a mirror.
She has the face of a child, somebody small, lunar.
Somebody's always standing by the bed. Sleep is the story
in which the child falls to the dead, rises, and is loved.

STANLEY PLUMLY

Product Warnings

To look at the warnings printed on virtually every product we buy, it would be fair to say that we consume at our own risk. While the many warning labels on a ladder, for example, are undoubtedly the fruit of liability suits, it is nevertheless unsettling to see them all there in yellow and red telling us not to "use on ice" or "lean against a power line."

Product warnings have their own clipped style. For example, a can of shaving cream shouts CONTENTS UNDER PRESSURE, rather than "The contents of this can are under pressure." When looked at with a writer's perspective, the gravity and drama of some of these warnings can be suggestive of other forms of creative writing. The following exercises ask you to play with these product warnings and see what might come from them.

Panning Instructions
Look at several product containers and instructions and make a list of warnings you find. Try mixing and matching some of the warnings in bizarre and humorous ways. See if you can write several sentences composed only of warnings, and be alert to possibilities for further development as poems, stories, or essays.

Excavating Instructions
Take this exercise a step further by exploring what happens when warnings are not heeded, as George Irving does in "Federal Offenses" (page 76). Consider also writing a love poem using only warnings, as in the poem "She Should Have Come with Warnings" (page 75).

♀ NUGGETS

Shawn Hall's poem "She Should Have Come with Warnings" (see below) developed out of the following list:

WARNING/CAUTION	PRODUCT
Use gentle strokes with a sharp razor. Contents under pressure. Do not puncture or incinerate. Do not heat for warm lather or any other purpose.	Barbasol
If rash or irritation develops, discontinue use. Do not apply to broken or irritated skin.	Shower To Shower (deodorant body powder)
Avoid spraying in eyes. Keep out of reach of children. Intentional misuse by deliberately concentrating and inhaling the contents can be harmful or fatal.	Aqua Net (hair spray)
Keep Away From Water Do not use while bathing. Always "Unplug It" after use	Vidal Sassoon Cold Shot 1500 Hair Dryer
May explode or leak, and cause burn injury, if recharged, disposed in a fire, mixed with different battery type, inserted backwards or disassembled.	Duracell Batteries
Burned out bulbs should be replaced quickly. Several burned out bulbs left in this set may cause the other bulbs to heat up and burn out.	Good Tidings Xmas Tree Lights

She Should Have Come with Warnings
Her eyes were as green
as the modern world
and just as toxic
when she cried. She should have come
with warnings.

When the rash
developed, I tried to discontinue
use, but by then
several bulbs had burned out
and I could not replace them.
The contents of her thoughts seemed always
under pressure. I thought they might
explode or leak
and cause burn injuries. Do not
puncture or incinerate, I thought.
Do not apply to broken skin.
Once she called me at work
in the middle of the day
to say only that she had drawn
a picture of my right hand
from a memory. Which one, I said,
but she hung up. Always unplug
after use. Use gentle strokes
with a sharp razor. Misuse may result
in sickness or death. She should have come
with warnings.

SHAWN HALL

 ## ARTIFACTS

From the short story "Federal Offenses"

Already I was an hour late for work. Taft would assume I had one of those epic Lost Weekends and was writhing under the spell of toxic DTs.

I lay there hugging my pillow, annoyed at myself for oversleeping and annoyed at the stiff tag protruding from under the pillowcase and scratching my cheek. **Under Penalty of Law This Tag Is Not To Be Removed**, it read. The tag tried to assure me that all new material consisted of polyester fiber. And then in very fine print, it listed statute codes and stamps from six different states, including the District of Columbia.

I tried to rip the tag off, but it was double stitched into the seam. I gave it another tug, and it came off, along with batting from the pillow and foam pellets. "Great. I killed the pillow," I said aloud, and strangely I felt that something of that order had happened, especially as the foam pellets continued to seep out. All the sleep that had taken place on those pellets, all the dreams they had absorbed. . . .

GEORGE IRVING

Down the Street

Getting Lost, Finding the Way

M ost of us have gotten lost on our way somewhere, whether to a place local or distant. Maybe you got lost one day taking a shortcut through your own familiar neighborhood or, more typically, found yourself wandering in circles through a strange and distant city. The experience of getting lost is inherently dramatic, regardless of how long it takes to find the way. Indeed, getting lost and finding the way is one of life's basic dramas.

Panning Instructions

Begin a poem, story, or piece of creative nonfiction about a time you got lost. Consider the whole experience: the point at which you realized you were lost (even before that: were there signs or forebodings that you might get lost?) and what you saw and experienced while you were lost and when you eventually found your way. To help you generate material, complete or develop with details the following statements:

1. Things weren't right even before I left (describe the "things").
2. I knew I was lost when . . .
3. I was lost, and to make matters worse . . .
4. If I hadn't gotten lost, I would (not) have . . .
5. While I was trying to find the way, I kept thinking . . .

Combine your responses, as Lorraine Smits did in "No Time" (page 79), and consider possible meanings of why you got lost. Maybe some part of you knew exactly what you were doing. Perhaps you weren't lost at all.

Excavating Instructions

Try doing the same exercise metaphorically. Instead of being lost with respect to an actual place, consider experiences in which you were intellectually lost or emotionally lost or spiritually lost. In the poem "This Is the Way" (on page 80), the last stanza suggests that the "founding fathers" were morally lost as well as geographically lost. Try using some of the same details and expressions from the first exercise.

NUGGETS

From the short story "No Time"

Fog swirled around. So thick at times even the white line on the road disappeared. You'll see signs, the man at the gas station had said. I had used up an eighth of a tank of gas and seen no sign. Wait! The fog wasn't quite so dense. Something was forming up ahead. A road sign. It looked so strange, though. A pale purple, almost pink. Points all around the edges like a misshapen star. The words were black and seemed to leap out—You Are Here. Here? Where is Here? I felt confused, the way I did last week in the Metro Station. I had stood in front of the map board trying to figure out which exit I wanted. The bright red star saying You Are Here hadn't helped at all. I still took the wrong escalator and walked blocks out of my way.

This road was so dark. When the fog was patchy, I saw trees crowding the sides, thick and woodsy. At times bare branches seemed to reach out and gather in the fog. It's a shortcut, the man had said. But the gas gauge had dropped below the halfway mark. Why does the unfamiliar seem so much longer and darker? My radio had shorted out on the way to the party. Took the clock with it. No friendly green eye to keep me company. No soothing voice to calm my uneasiness.

Lorraine Smits

ARTIFACTS

From the short story "A Good Man Is Hard to Find"

They turned onto the dirt road and the car raced roughly along in a swirl of pink dust. The grandmother recalled the times when there were no paved roads and thirty miles was a day's journey. The dirt road was hilly and there were sudden curves on dangerous embankments. All at once they would be on a hill, looking down over the blue tops of trees for miles around, then the next minute, they would be in a red depression with the dust-coated trees looking down on them.

"This place had better turn up in a minute," Bailey said, "or I'm going to turn around."

Flannery O'Connor

From the memoir *Remembering the Bone House*

Another day, Sally and I get lost in earnest. We've been mistreated by one or more of the women in that high white house, each of whom confers power on the others, and for once we're making good on our threat to run away. We stomp right off Lindall Hill and into town. This would have been the familiar territory of Mother's adolescence, which I will read about in a few years, during my own adolescence, in a diary she lets me see. She walked to high school through these streets, and wandered through them after school with her friends, especially her boyfriend Darren, whom she might have married, thereby eradicating me from her future and my own tenuous present. . . . Sally and I wander past streets of houses and on into the business district, clutching hands, increasingly confused and nervous. Being together protects us from panic, however, as though we can never go really, truly irrevocably astray in the world unless we lose each other. We're even a little titillated to be having the experience we've so often been warned against: Getting Lost.

NANCY MAIRS

This Is the Way
We are only a little
lost. Any minute
our destination will appear
around the next hill, past one more
light. Let's just see. Sure

we could clear this up
at the Texaco station on the corner
but doing so lacks gusto and style.
If we have to ask others in times
like this, where are we? More lost
than we are now, I say, even though we're

hours late and haven't seen asphalt in miles,
even though we're running out of gas
and the passengers are skeletons
who died of uremic poisoning
when their bladders burst. Still

this is the best method. This
is the way our fathers
and forefathers, lost for months
crazed with their own conversations
drinking salt water and eating
their slaves, found America.

MICHAEL C. SMITH

Excuses, Excuses, Excuses

Some of the most important fiction and poetry evolves out of crunch situations in which deadlines are missed, promises are not kept, or mistakes are made (always in the passive voice). The genre is that of the Excuse. Whether the dog ate the homework, there were traffic jams of biblical proportions, or someone needed to be rescued from the office shredding machine, excuses almost always blend the plausible with the highly implausible.

The following exercise provides some hypothetical situations and asks you to invent excuses, and then to develop your excuses into a poem, story, or essay.

Panning Instructions

In the following exercise, for one of the situations in the left column, invent an excuse using one or more of the items in the right column, and develop the result into a poem or story.

Situation	Potential Culprits
A woman misses her flight by an hour.	bread
	a dog
A college student oversleeps and misses a final exam in a chemistry class.	the moon
	stockings
	a radio
Your mortgage payment is two weeks late.	a bed
	a head of cabbage
You missed your mate's birthday.	algebra
You greeted someone familiar using the wrong name.	a hubcap
	bad milk
You ran a red light.	dust
	the toilet

Excavating Instructions

When we find ourselves making the same excuse for some things we missed, forgot, or neglected—or when we almost habitually forget someone's birthday, anniversary, or name, there may be more to it than we want to admit.

Not all slips are Freudian, but unquestionably unconscious motives sometimes translate into embarrassing behaviors.

Begin a story or poem wherein an excuse breaks down finally and someone is forced to grapple with the truth behind the excuse. The character can come to this point herself, or it might come out as a result of being challenged by someone.

☗ NUGGETS

From a short story in progress

She arrived breathless at the American Airlines check-in counter, her flight long gone. The man behind the counter smiled as she approached.

"Looks like you're a little late," he said.

"Yes," she said. "Is it possible to get on another flight?"

"Yes, it is possible. But you'll need to purchase another ticket."

There was no way she could instantly come up with the money to buy another ticket. It had taken her six months to save up for this ticket.

"Look," she said, "I missed my flight because of the airline—or at least the airport."

The man looked puzzled.

"Your bathroom flooded. A toilet ran over."

"But I don't see . . ." the man started to say.

"I tried to find someone to fix it. I looked everywhere for someone," she said.

"But that doesn't . . . I mean we're grateful, but. . . ."

She sensed that she had him on the ropes—or at least had him backing into a corner.

"What if one of your customers slipped on that floor? Think of the injuries. The law suits. I thought about them, for you, for your airline. On your behalf, and now I've missed my flight." She began to sob.

The man looked genuinely sympathetic.

"But ma'am," he said. "That was an hour ago."

AMANDA SHELDON

 **ARTIFACTS**

This Is Just to Say
I have eaten
the plums
that were in
the icebox

and which
you were probably saving
for breakfast

Forgive me
they were delicious
so sweet
so cold

WILLIAM CARLOS WILLIAMS

Caught Up in the News

D aily we are bombarded by news from myriad sources—newspapers, magazines, TV, radio, Internet. We absorb much more information than we can possibly use, and all the irrelevant information gets mixed up with the relevant. Why do we need to know about another car accident, murder, wonderful accomplishment by a celebrity athlete, or the passage of a bill that affects six people in Alaska?

The following exercises encourage you to make creative use of all this news by incorporating it in your own writing—to indeed look for more news and use it in creative ways.

Panning Instructions

Look through several issues of newspapers and magazines and copy down leads and headlines that strike you as provocative, amusing, or absurd. Link the leads together in semilogical ways. For example, Anita Perez took the following leads from the July 6, 1994, edition of *The Washington Post* and produced the plausible sentences below to begin a story.

- The all talk, no help labels on bottles
- U.S. to bar Haitians picked up at sea
- Labrador lovers unleash their anger
- Battered woman's cry relayed up from grass roots
- Bus repair pact scrapped
- Boy devours books
- What Popeye didn't know
- Name two sports with no clear goals

The women unleashed their anger because the United States barred the all talk, no help labels on Haitians.

Popeye didn't know that devouring books is better than devouring grass roots and spinach.

The bus of battered labradors was scrapped because it had no clear goals.

She chose the first sentence to help her begin her story about two women who meet while waiting to see their senator (see below).

☀ Excavating Instructions

Combine excerpts from several stories in different newspapers and magazines in a story, poem, or essay. Feel free to add your own connections and language. Notice how the excerpt from Ron Carlson's story, "Reading the Paper" (below), creates a strange effect by combining ordinary, daily details and behaviors with details drawn from the newspaper.

🜂 NUGGETS

From a story in progress

Two women, who did not know each other, met outside of Senator Bradley's office to unleash their anger about the administration's policy toward Haitians. They were particularly upset about all the talk and the lack of aid. The women didn't know that the senator was in Colorado. In the course of the five hours they waited, they got to know each other quite well.

ANITA PEREZ

☉ ARTIFACTS

From the story "Reading the Paper"

All I want to do is read the paper, but I've got to do the wash first. There's blood all over everything. Duke and the rest of the family except me were killed last night by a drunk driver, run over in a movie line, and this blood is not easy to get out. Most of the fabrics are easy to clean, however, so I don't even bother reading the fine print on the Cheer box. They make this soap to work in all conditions anymore. Then I get Timmy up and ready for school. He eats two Hostess doughnuts and before he's even down the street and I've picked up the paper, I can hear him screaming down there. Somebody's dragging him into a late model Datsun, light brown, the kind of truck Duke, bless his soul, always thought was silly. So, I've got the paper in my hands and there's someone at the door. So few people come to the back door that I know it's going to be something odd, and I'm right. It's that guy in the paper who escaped from prison yesterday. He wants to know if he can come in and rape me and cut me up a little bit. Well, after he does that, my coffee's cold, so I pour a new cup.

RON CARLSON

Neighborly and Unneighborly Neighbors

With the fragmentation of our culture and its inherent value of individualism and privacy, the status and role of our neighbors are by no means assured. For all those who like and trust their neighbors and consider them beloved relatives, there are just as many who keep a safe and frosty distance from them, fearing that they will borrow and break the lawn mower or want to learn more about their neighbors' lives than they have a right to know.

Regardless of our personal experiences as neighbors, there are things each of us would do with our neighbors and things each of us most emphatically would not do—all for reasons as personal as they are logical. "Good fences make good neighbors," said Robert Frost, and when those fences, both physical and psychological, are violated, conflicts arise.

In this next exercise, you're asked to examine the fences between neighbors and to explore the feelings associated with them and with the fact that we all live next to someone, whether he or she is in the apartment next door or on a farm three miles down the road.

Panning Instructions

1. Make a **list** of items you would never lend to a neighbor, mixing the typical with the bizarre—for example, my razor, my car, my shoes, my underwear, my husband.

2. Write a piece in which you are asked and actually lend one of the bizarre items to the neighbor. Discuss the shape this item was in before you lent it and the shape it was in when it was returned. For an essay approach to this exercise, recall and describe a time a neighbor actually asked to borrow something you weren't completely comfortable lending.

Excavating Instructions

1. Sometimes our neighbors create other kinds of conflicts for us. They park a new BMW in their driveway and suddenly our Subaru looks old and ragged. Our carefully transplanted azaleas all die while their rhododendrons cause people to slow down and gawk. Write a piece that takes off on the theme of

"Keeping Up with the Joneses" the way that Raymond Carver does in the first paragraph of his short story "Neighbors" (see page 89). Explore the tension that arises from falling behind the Joneses in some area, perhaps in an absurd way. ("We didn't even own an artist, much less a celebrity, so when the Wilsons bought Madonna and brought her home, we hid our faces and vowed to catch up.")

2. Write a piece from the point of view of a neighbor and explore some of the conclusions the neighbor might make about you and your family.

3. Begin a poem, story, or essay about a neighbor whose actions and behavior are mysterious in some way. For example, what questions would naturally arise in the situation described in the poem "Duplex" by James Washington (page 88)?

🕺 NUGGETS

neither a borrower nor a lender be

my neighbor says may i borrow your
guillotine this evening   i'm
having a party i need
something to amuse the guests

i have i don't mind saying
the keenest guillotine
on the block but
i'm canny   who

'll be using it i said
not
that thickneck brotherinlaw of yours
who broke my radial arm saw trimming
his leg

he never meant it
my neighbor whines   how
would he know that bone
would be so tough and   furthermore

i said i just had
that guillotine in the shop she's
not so young anymore   only
licensed operators he insists (unlike

that incident with my B-17 bomber
and his dirtbag
cousin from the eastern shore)   no
hotdogging it i exhort   we

put up the garage door
and wheel that beauty
into the midday sun   and
back tomorrow morning ten o'clock

sharp

which he does
all clean and oiled along
with brotherinlaw's soccerball
head

on my mother's
best china plate

Liz Enagonio

Duplex

The man next door keeps kicking
at the wall we have in common.
There is a rhythm to it, faster
than raindrops, slower
than heartbeats. At first I thought
it was a code, but the intervals
are so regular that if it is a code
he is saying the same thing over and over.
Given the conditions of this duplex, he
is probably repeating in code the name
of his god. I would complain
but the rent is low,
and anyway I've gotten caught up
in the rhythm. If my life were a scull,
the pounding on the wall would tell me
when to rest and when to row.

James Washington

ARTIFACTS

From the short story "Neighbors"

Bill and Arlene Miller were a happy couple. But now and then they felt they alone among their circle had been passed by somehow, leaving Bill to attend to his bookkeeping duties and Arlene occupied with secretarial chores. They talked about it sometimes, mostly in comparison with the lives of their neighbors, Harriet and Jim Stone. It seemed to the Millers that the Stones lived a fuller and brighter life. The Stones were always going out for dinner, or entertaining at home, or traveling about the country somewhere in connection with Jim's work.

RAYMOND CARVER

From the short story "The Neighbor"

Country people can forgive madness, but a week ago, the family's one immediate neighbor, a dour young man in his twenties, had walked out his back door and had seen, for the tenth time, one of their chickens scratching in his pathway to the woodpile. He'd rushed back into the house, and returning with an Army .45 handgun, had fired eight bullets into the chicken, making a feathered, bloody mess.

RUSSELL BANKS

Customs and the Customary

In parts of Spain, when a person compliments someone on a possession, say a large watercolor hanging on the wall, the host/owner may offer the possession to the guest. If the guest politely declines the offer, the host may insist all the more and take it as an insult if the guest does not accept. In Japan, it is considered the height of rudeness to touch a stranger's head. In the United States, strangers will often inquire about each other's occupation as a way of breaking the ice. These are all examples of customs—habitual or ritualized behaviors practiced by discrete groups—and they may or may not have any basis in reason or rationality. And since there is no necessary connection between customs and reason, this is an area rich in creative writing possibilities.

Panning Instructions

1. Select a few of the following areas and generate a **list** of customs associated with each:

- Eating/Meals/Restaurants
- Public Transportation
- Weddings
- Parties
- Funerals
- Public Restrooms
- Holidays
- Greetings
- Farewells
- Sporting Events
- Dress/Fashion
- Romance
- Kissing (see the example essay on page 91)

2. Begin a poem, story, or essay that involves conflicts related to these customs, for example, the man from Albania who gets in a crowded elevator and faces rearward for twelve floors. Or consider the kind of trouble a man might get into by not observing the custom of kissing a woman's hands, a custom Michael T. Kaufman's essay challenges (see below).

Excavating Instructions

Try your hand at inventing your own customs for some of the areas mentioned above. Remember: these customs don't need to make any sense. Use the customs you invent in a poem, story, or essay. Notice how Dorothy Nims's poem "My House" blends and takes off on actual customs (below).

NUGGETS

My House

In my house you must remove your shoes
and place them on your hands. Once
conversation begins, you may drop one
at a time to punctuate what
you are saying. In my house
you must try to draw a picture of me
and tell me why this is how you see me.
(All such efforts hang on the Great Wall, signed
and dated.) Here, no mention is ever made
of presidents, dead or living. You are expected
to rise when I rise, place a hand on my shoulder
and walk with me to the bathroom. In my house
the most venerable custom is the great dance
that takes places upon leaving: we embrace
as in a tango, re-trace our steps and conversations
and move out of the house, where I stop
turn, and you are
gone.

DOROTHY NIMS

ARTIFACTS

From the essay "Kissing Customs"

I returned not long ago from a three-year assignment in Poland, where men kiss the hands of women as a matter of course when they meet. When I first arrived in Warsaw, I did not think this was such a great idea. At the time I thought of myself as a democratic kid from the streets of New York, and the notion of bending over and brushing my lips over the back of a woman's hand struck me as offensively feudal and hopelessly effete. Each time some perfectly fine woman offered me the back of her hand to kiss, I stammered my apology, saying something like, "Gosh, no offense intended, but where I come from we don't carry on like this, and while I respect you enormously, can't we make do with a simple handshake?"

MICHAEL T. KAUFMAN

Building Codes and Zones

If you own or have owned a house, then at one time or another you have encountered the laws of property use. From the surprising discovery that the house you dearly want to sell has electrical wiring from the age of Edison (read: below code) to the dismaying fact that the 100-foot-tall dead elm tree by the road belongs to you and not to the city, the perils of home ownership are manifold. Even as renters, we are affected by nuances in building codes and zones. You find out too late, for example, that the pricey apartment you rented with a view of the ocean also came with the noise of a nearby reggae bar, or that your water pressure was intimately affected by everyone else's shower and toilet behavior.

All of these collisions of life and the code involve conflicts and usually strong language. The following exercises ask you to launch stories, poems, or essays that, in one way or another, center on how laws affect the spaces we inhabit.

Panning Instructions

1. Try creating a list of strange building or construction codes and use them to launch a poem or story. For example: Standard bathrooms must have two facing toilets. Hot water heaters must have names. Every house in town is required to have a view of something "interesting," and it is up to the contractor to say what it will be.

2. Try developing a poem or story that opens with the following sentence: For over two weeks he had been delivering water to this neighborhood, but just today he noticed what all the houses had in common, though there was nothing common about it.

3. Create a list of responses to the following prompt and then develop a poem, story, or essay based on it: Just as the realtor had said, the house was almost perfect. If it weren't for _____, it would be perfect.

Excavating Instructions

While building codes and zones presumably evolve through some democratic process involving communities and neighborhoods, the aspects, elements, and locations of where we choose to live also involve our personal preferences and histories. Just as your city may require that all fuse boxes be able to accommodate at least 20 amps of current, your own fuse box or your tolerance for noise, pollution, traffic, children, and so forth has its own very personal capacity, which will likely have more to do with what you have experienced and expect than with any objective criteria.

Begin a story, poem, or essay that focuses on the conflicts of self and location. For example, a man chooses an apartment without input from his wife and it has everything except the one thing she cherishes and needs: light or space or charm or angles. You choose. Or a couple picks an apartment ideal for them but in many ways terrible for the child they are expecting.

🖐 NUGGETS

A View Without a Room

For walls
we have windows.
The Golden Gate bridge spans
bedroom and living room.
For chandeliers
we have speckled galls.
For carpet, the razor-waved
bay. We love light
and light is everywhere. Yet,

our breathing is a tunnel
so narrow I'm not sure
whose heart just beat
or whose stomach just growled
or who's the shadow and who
the shape that carves it. This could be

exquisite no matter how you cut
exquisite.

Were you ever in prison?
I should know the answer and would
if you were only
a roommate or a priest. Good that we each
got a key and good that we're not
the kind of people who keep
animals.

Kim Cheong

 **ARTIFACTS**

From the short story "Bereaved Apartments"

Gilbert McClure is the man she shares a house with, in a manner of speaking. It's divided, the way a house can be split down the middle when a landlord sees how he could get twice the rent for the same piece of pie, and makes it a duplex. *There's doors that go right through between my bedroom and his living room, but they're nailed shut and painted over,* she writes Aunt Reima. *Mr. McClure's side must have got the real kitchen because mine's a closet with a hot plate. But it went vice versa on the bathrooms.* And Aunt Reima writes back that yes she's heard those called "love's losts" or some people say "bereaved apartments," because, she supposes, each one is missing something it once had.

BARBARA KINGSOLVER

"I Would Have Burned My Hair for That Waitress"

Occupying a place between lovers and parents, our good friends know how to see the world the way we see it and know when that vision is distorted. It is their job to provide reality checks—to let us know, for example, that the bell-bottoms don't evoke the charm of the flower age, as the salesperson led us to believe, or to dull the glitz on that no-load mutual fund we have been thinking could nicely replace our profit sharing.

Truly good friends hold a position of utter trust because they like us for who we are, and they don't usually have as great a stake as lovers and parents in making us feel good for the sake of feeling good or making us feel bad because whatever action we have taken or are considering taking might have a direct effect on their lives.

For some, trust between friends is nearly sacred, and when that trust is broken—when a friend tells a shared secret or purposely offers us poor advice—our feeling of betrayal does not usually fade easily. While our friends can be our greatest allies, they can also become our most difficult rivals as we test the confines of these relationships and measure our own successes and failures in relationship to theirs.

Panning Instructions

1. Cluster on the words *friendship* and *trust*. Combine your "balloons" in a variety of ways in an attempt to make surprising connections.

2. Begin a story, poem, or essay involving a secret or a specific trust between two friends—you and a friend, people you know, or fictional characters. The secret should challenge the boundaries of the friendship in some way. You might explore a time that you told a confidence to a friend as a way of testing the level of this friendship, or you might write about a time that a friend became less of a friend by breaking an important trust or more of a friend by keeping a trust. Notice how a friendship is affirmed when one friend lies for another in "A Year of Living Stupidly" (page 97).

Excavating Instructions

While we usually trust our friends to be tactfully honest with us, they may not always live up to our expectations. Jealousy may cause a friend to tell you that your hair looks terrific dyed black when in fact you look like Morticia Addams on a bad day. A sense of competition may cause you to fail to remind a friend to study for an upcoming quiz.

Work on a story, essay, or poem about a time when either a friend's lack of honesty or your lack of honesty toward a friend caused a conflict in your life. The conflict may have been external (causing a fight between the two of you or others) or may have remained internal (causing you guilt or anxiety).

NUGGETS

Taking Orders

I would have burned my hair
for this waitress, so full and good
were her thoughts, so tempered
her voice, and my friend knew this, so that
when I ordered the coffee
and she asked "Will there be
anything else?" my friend
answered for me so I wouldn't have
to stutter my "no thanks"
and spend all day collecting myself.

MARTIN RODRIGUEZ

From the short story "A Year of Living Stupidly"

Those last few weeks in Vietnam were the hardest. I totally bought into the fear that afflicted most short timers: that Charlie knew when you were shipping out and waited for your year in hell to almost end before pulling your number. So I spent a lot of time in the mortar bunker. Telford knew I was scared shitless and would take over for me on the radios when terror so seized me that I couldn't function. And when Sarge asked him where I was, he'd tell him stories—that I was in Phu Heip getting supplies or at the Korean command post dropping off bombing reports. Two days before I shipped out, the Sarge wandered into the bunker around noon, and saw me squatting there among those mildewed sandbags. He said, "You know, your friend Telford thinks you're in the village. Better tell him you're down here."

They all knew what I was going through. Everybody fell victim to superstition the last weeks. And that was okay.

MIKE BRITZ

 # ARTIFACTS

Picking Blackberries with a Friend
Who Has Been Reading Jacques Lacan

August is dust here. Drought
stuns the road,
but juice gathers in the berries.

We pick them in the hot
slow-motion of midmorning.
Charlie is exclaiming:

for him it is twenty years ago
and raspberries and Vermont.
We have stopped talking

about *L'Histoire de la vérité*,
about subject and object
and the mediation of desire.

Our ears are stoppered
in the bee-hum. And Charlie,
laughing wonderfully,

beard stained purple
by the word *juice,*
goes to get a bigger pot.

ROBERT HASS

Community Service

How many times do we hear of some famous person being sentenced to 300 hours of community service for reckless driving or 80 hours of community service for getting into a fist fight in a restaurant in front of twelve camera crews?

Some of us serve our communities out of pride and perhaps even love for our neighborhoods and neighbors. We enthusiastically run for city offices and volunteer at recreation centers and schools. Still, the majority of us find ourselves sentenced in some way to community service, if not officially by the law, then unofficially by friends and circumstances that demand our involvement.

While community involvement is certainly a good thing (it could even be argued that our neighborhoods really exist only because some citizens have it in them to start newsletters, organize block parties, and maintain neighborhood watch programs), community projects also bring out a certain zeal in some that can be overwhelming. No matter how burdened we may feel by their presence and requests for assistance, when we encounter those who possess this zeal, the interactions we have are rife with creative possibilities.

Panning Instructions

1. Think back to a time when someone asked you to get involved in a neighborhood or civic cause. Perhaps a dorm-mate tried to enlist your help in setting up a building security plan or a neighbor asked you to sign a petition to get a traffic light installed. Or in the fifth grade you somehow found yourself volunteering as a crossing guard for a month. **Freewrite** about this service, generating all the details you can remember about it and the invitation to get involved. If you are now heavily involved in neighborhood causes, choose one or two that you are most active in and trace your involvement.

2. Recall the person who asked you to become involved or with whom you closely work in your community project. What physical traits (for example, tall and thin, slightly crossed eyes) and personality markers (such as eager laugh, twitchy eyebrow) does she possess? List all that you can recall.

3. Work on a story, poem, or essay that explores your encounter with community involvement. If you're working on fiction, feel free to alter and add characters. If you're working on an essay, try sorting through your motives for either getting involved or not getting involved. Mine the material for possible dramatic and comic potential, as Shirley Hickman does in her story "Neighborhood Watch" (below).

Excavating Instructions

Just as we serve or neglect our communities, our communities can serve us or fail to serve us in crucial ways. In one neighborhood, mail may be delivered irregularly without explanation; in another, the police may seem to spend their time reading magazines at the 7-Eleven instead of patrolling the streets. While we may be annoyed at the inconveniences caused by whatever disservice we experience, irritation can be turned into creative energy.

Begin a story, poem, or essay about a time that you experienced an interruption or complication in whatever community service you had come to expect in your life—perhaps the garbage collectors went on strike or the newspaper deliverer didn't wrap your paper in plastic when it rained—or maybe several services went haywire at the same time. Whatever the incident you choose to focus on, be sure to explore any comic or other emotional potential.

NUGGETS

From the story in progress "Neighborhood Watch"
"But I don't know anything about suspicious characters," I told Irene.

She assured me I didn't need to know much and that mainly we just drove around in the wee hours in a warm jeep with a two-way radio.

"Usually," she said, "we don't see anything except maybe a family of raccoons invading a garbage can. They're very cute."

"How 'wee'?" I asked.

"Between midnight and three, and it's only once a month."

"Just to report raccoons?"

"Oh," said Irene, smiling. "Sometimes we call in husbands late in getting home."

"Is that legal?" I asked.

"I don't know," Irene confessed. "But it sure is fun."

SHIRLEY HICKMAN

Power Lines

The year they stopped trimming back the trees
you moved away. I couldn't see you go through
the leaves but there had been rumors about it.
We all worried about power line
fires after you left. The children who played
in your deserted front yard lost kites
in the branches. When the new family moved in
none of us invited them over. I'm sorry I
didn't go to his funeral. I have a photograph
from before it happened. My kids on his lap—
the neighborhood's Grandpop. If you left a
forwarding address, I'd be happy to send it.

DELORES QUIGLEY

 ARTIFACTS

From the short story "The Longest Day of the Year"

Toward the end of my third marriage, when my husband and I had enough problems on our hands, the Welcome Wagon lady began to call on us. It was just a rented house—more than we could afford, too, so we were going to have to give it up before summer was over. The first time she came I told her it was an inconvenient time to talk, and that we were going to be moving, anyway. Still, she came back the next day, saying that she hoped I had a minute. That day had been hell. . . . I had to tell her that it wasn't a good time. Not to be put off, she asked when it would be. . . .

The next week she came back. She was a tall woman, quite heavy, wearing a white poncho with black stars woven into the wool and ratty-looking fur tails. She had on a black skirt that I knew the dog would get hairs all over, and a ring on her wedding finger that looked like something Richard Burton would have bought Elizabeth Taylor. It was so large that the diamond had fallen side-ways, and rested against her baby finger. She was trying to flick it straight when I opened the door. . . .

"As you can probably tell, I love this community and want to serve it," she said.

ANN BEATTIE

The Road Not Taken

The Road Not Taken

Two roads diverged in a yellow wood,
And sorry I could not travel both
And be one traveler, long I stood
And looked down one as far as I could
To where it bent in the undergrowth;

Then took the other, as just as fair,
And having perhaps the better claim,
Because it was grassy and wanted wear;
Though as for that, the passing there
Had worn them really about the same,

And both that morning equally lay
In leaves no step had trodden black.
Oh, I kept the first for another day!
Yet knowing how way leads on to way,
I doubted if I should ever come back.

I shall be telling this with a sigh
Somewhere ages and ages hence:
Two roads diverged in a wood, and I—
I took the one less traveled by,
And that has made all the difference.

ROBERT FROST

Robert Frost's poem alludes to all the important choices we make in our lives and laments that we cannot "travel both." The poem concludes that the choice the narrator makes "has made all the difference," which might be said of any and all significant choices we make. At one time or another, most of us have speculated about the roads we did not take, not necessarily in regret but perhaps in simple wonder of what might have been. If you had married that other person—the football player, the rebel, the prom queen, the Goody Two Shoes—what would your life have been like? If you had stuck with engineering instead of going into marketing, where would you be? The following exercises encourage you to incorporate these speculations into your writing, to take off on them or develop them as your whim dictates.

𝕏 Panning Instructions

Make a list of five tough choices you have faced in your life. Select one, and **freewrite** on why this was a difficult choice. Think about the option you didn't choose, and make a **list** tabulating the imaginary chain of consequences that might have resulted if you had chosen this alternative. Draft a detailed portrait, in the third person, of the self you would be right now had you followed the alternative path. Pursue this as a poem, story, or essay, depending on where it leads you. In his poignant poem "Reunion in the Donut Shop," Bryan Pendargast imagines only a temporary reprieve from his fate and that of an old flame he runs into (see below).

🔦 Excavating Instructions

The narrator in Frost's poem chooses to take "the road less traveled," the road that veers off the beaten path. Which of the choices you have made fall in this category? What were the least "popular" of your choices? In an essay, a story about a fictional character, or a poem, explore the conflicts that arise by not taking the well-worn path.

🕴 NUGGETS

Reunion in the Donut Shop
Twenty-two years. She looked her age
in the fluorescence
of Dunkin' Donuts. I could have saved her
from that. She could have saved me
from irony, her checkered-table cloth sense
of humor, a light on
in each of her eyes. So many nights
we sat above the city
in my black Mercury

we thought we were gods. We would have had
six kids and a dozen TVs, a Jesus
in every window, and for all that a short
time of it.

BRYAN PENDARGAST

 ## ARTIFACTS

From the novel *In the Night Cafe*

One morning on Seventh Street I woke up and looked around that small room. It was already getting crowded with rolled-up canvases. I stared at your brush marks on the walls. The floorboards were dappled with color; the May air smelled of turpentine. We were living inside your painting. I had a thought that took me by surprise. I am in my life. My real life had surrounded me. What I wanted was exactly what I had.

That was the moment, I think, when I finally gave up on the theater. It wasn't even painful. It just made sense. I saw it was what I had to do. I just decided to give you what you needed. I wanted to do it so quietly, though, you wouldn't even catch me at it.

JOYCE JOHNSON

The Backpack

Whether we carry a knapsack, pocketbook, briefcase, diaper bag, or some kind of combination of the four, many of us have trouble getting out of the house without taking some of our possessions with us. While someone totes work she hopes to do when traveling back and forth to her office, another person slips a novel into her purse in case the bus is late again. Like turtles, we tend to carry part of our world on our backs (or shoulders).

Although much of what we take with us out into the world every day is practical and necessary, hidden among the sensible calculators, notebooks, and diapers are less functional possessions, curiosities that represent the more complex realities of our daily lives.

Panning Instructions

1. Empty everything from your pocketbook, briefcase, knapsack, or baby's diaper bag onto a clean surface. (This exercise works even better if you do this with a friend.) Everything. Even that mouldy-looking saltine holds valuable clues. (Don't throw anything away—yet.) If you don't carry a bag or pack on a regular basis, empty your wallet of everything, even that ATM receipt you forgot to record in your checkbook.

2. Move back a few steps to gain perspective and look at all these items as someone in search of clues about your life, as an anthropologist or a detective might look at them. Try not to judge. (All thoughts that begin with the phrase, "I can't believe I still have that stupid _____ " should be immediately banished.)

Forget for the moment that these are your things, and try to imagine that they belong to someone else. What do these items tell you about this person? (For example, several gum wrappers might suggest a nervous person; several little mirrors, a narcissistic person; several kinds of pills, a hypochondriac.) What one item among all the possessions in front of you are you most surprised to discover? (Why have you held on to that lottery ticket so long?)

3. Using these telling items as a starting point, begin a story, poem, or essay about the person whose life you have laid out before you. In the excerpt from Perri Klass's short story, "A Gift of Sweet Mustard" (page 107), notice how a jar of champagne honey mustard tells us a great deal about Alan as a husband.

☀ Excavating Instructions

Look back at the item that you discovered that most surprised you. It may be something seemingly inconsequential—someone else's business card—or seemingly more meaningful—a therapist's phone number or the wedding band you no longer wear. Often we carry things with us when we aren't sure where else to keep them or when we aren't yet ready to get rid of them. Even a dingy-looking after-dinner mint stuck to the bottom of a purse might serve to subconsciously remind someone about a much-enjoyed and long-ago night on the town.

Begin a story, poem, or essay that explores the significance of the item that most surprised you. In the excerpt from Angelin Donohue's story in progress, a single mother has to do some fast thinking to account for the toy in her purse. She doesn't yet want the man she is interested in to know that she has children (see page 107). Try completing the following sentences for triggers to get started:

1. Probably she wasn't the only person who carried a _____ (water pistol, photograph of David Bowie, and so on) with her to _____ (work, school, and so on), but she knew it wasn't likely that she'd find out who else did.

2. It didn't even mean anything to me anymore, but there it was anyway, _____ (her father's phone number, an accident lawyer's card, and so forth) accompanying me everywhere I went.

3. At first I was surprised to find _____ (his phone number, my old prescription card, and so on) in my _____, but maybe I really did intend to keep it.

☂ NUGGETS

From a short story in progress

Megan hadn't meant to mislead Alan when the plastic dinosaur had fallen out of her purse. It was just that she had seen his office, with its clutter of political cartoons, his hanging rubber stork, pink slinky and other miscellaneous anti-establishment toys, and wanted him to know that she wasn't buying into the system either. So, when Alan picked it up and said "Cool," and handed the Brachiosaurus back to her with a new glimmer of recognition in his eye, she hadn't found it necessary to tell him that the toy belonged to her son, and that she had only this morning rescued it from under his car seat.

Mostly she was relieved that her purse hadn't been dumped in front of him the year before when there would have been baby wipes and a spare pacifier mixed in with the usual wallet, checkbook and keys. She decided now, today, was definitely a better time.

ANGELIN DONOHUE

 ## ARTIFACTS

From the short story "A Gift of Sweet Mustard"

In his briefcase is a jar of champagne honey mustard. He has bought it partly to celebrate his own goodness as a husband; at work the blond California Girl who works in the next office had dropped in on him for a chat and suggested they go somewhere after work for a drink. Alan said he couldn't, he had to be somewhere. Of course, he didn't say he had to get home to his wife, which is what a really good husband would surely have said. No one at work knows he is married. . . .

Alan is thinking about the champagne honey mustard, and how Joanna will try a little on the end of her finger and then spread it all over her share of whatever they are having for dinner.

PERRI KLASS

Around the Water Cooler

Many of us scorn gossips, imagining ourselves above listening to or spreading rumors about other people's lives. Yet, we cannot help tuning in when a man behind us on the bus discusses his therapy session with a friend. And not many of us can resist listening to whatever tidbit follows the phrase "Do you promise to keep this a secret?"

Sometimes gossip is just gossip, a generally harmless distraction from our routines. But intimacies about other people's lives can wake us up to our own desires and fears, forcing us to question the choices we are making in our own lives. For example, while we may judge the secretary who is rumored to be sleeping with her boss, we also may be privately impressed with the risks she is taking, with how willing she seems to gain or lose so much.

Panning Instructions

1. What gossip (unsubstantiated claims about events, things, or people) have you heard or helped to spread in the past year? Who told you the gossip? To help remember, think about your regular weekly routines and make a list of different areas of your life in which you might hear gossip, as in the list below. If you can't remember hearing gossip in any of the places, write a question mark.

Location	Gossip Heard
Jake's daycare	New teacher pregnant and going to quit—don't remember who said.
The carpool	??
At work	Merger? Everyone says lunch hour is going to be shortened to a half-hour.
Night school	Woman who sits next to me told me that the final exam is the same as the practice test in the back of our book.
Evie's Brownie troop meetings	??

2. Add to your **Gossip Heard** column by inventing likely and bizarre rumors. Be sure to incorporate any fantasies you harbor about people, as in the list below.

Location	Gossip Heard
Jake's daycare	New teacher pregnant and going to quit—don't remember who said. **Tuition increase is really paying for teacher's other wardrobe in her secret life as an exotic dancer.**
The carpool	?? **Kathryn has been ten minutes late each day this week because she is secretly doing a paper route in the mornings to pay off debts.**
At work	Merger? Everyone says lunch hour is going to be shortened to a half-hour. ??
Night school	Woman who sits next to me told me that the final exam is the same as the practice test in the back of our book. **Noisy class across the hall is really a singles' meeting and not a credit class at all.**
Evie's Brownie troop meetings	?? **Cookies this year contain secret chemical that makes everyone feel love for their country as soon as they take a bite.**

3. Begin a story, poem, or essay that incorporates some of the "real" and invented gossip from your list. Treat all of it as fact. For an essay approach to this exercise, explain why you believe that both the "real" gossip and rumors you invented are believable.

Excavating Instructions

What gossip might someone spread about you? What gossip would you least like to have spread about yourself? Go back to your list one more time and invent rumors about yourself that reflect your worries about the way others see you. Then add these new rumors to the piece you are working on. If you're writing an essay, examine your motives for inventing this gossip about yourself. Why are you afraid other people see you this way? See the examples in the **Gossip Heard** column below.

Location	Gossip Heard
Jake's daycare	New teacher pregnant and going to quit—don't remember who said.
	Tuition increase is really paying for teacher's other wardrobe in her secret life as an exotic dancer.
	Teachers talk about how I'm a neglectful mother— why does he always have food stains on his face and clothes?
The carpool	??
	Kathryn has been ten minutes late each day this week because she is secretly doing a paper route in the mornings to pay off debts.
	On the Wednesdays that I'm off, they probably gossip about how rundown I'm looking, and our house is looking, lately—wonder if we're having money troubles.
At work	Merger? Everyone says lunch hour is going to be shortened to a half-hour.
	??
	Coworkers discuss the possibility of me getting fired for losing that account last month.
Night school	Woman who sits next to me told me that the final exam is the same as the practice test in the back of our book.
	Noisy class across the hall is really a singles' meeting and not a credit class at all.
	Teenagers who sit in the back gossip about my stupid middle-aged haircut.
Evie's Brownie troop meetings	???
	Cookies this year contain secret chemical that makes everyone feel love for their country as soon as they take a bite.
	??

 # NUGGETS

From the essay "That's a Fact"

Rumor has it that the stock market is going to crash. At least this is what my brother Thomas claims. He's getting a divorce or at least that's what Marcia told me. Marcia's the woman who does my nails. She does my sister-in-law's, too. Or should I say ex-sister-in-law? Not that I ever liked her that much. My brother was always a step above her on the evolution ladder. Marcia was abducted by space aliens when she was eighteen. This is, in my opinion, the one thing that makes her interesting. She showed me the exact spot she was standing in her backyard when they swooped down to get her. You don't even want to hear the details because, let me tell you, they're not very pretty. Her backyard was built over a swamp. This whole town was built on a swamp. That's why our grass is like a sponge after one brief rain shower. Don't even bother trying to find any land records to prove this. They were all burned a long time ago. In that terrible fire. The one that happened well before I got here, if you believe my Uncle Albert.

RITA MATERSON

 # ARTIFACTS

From the short story "Glossolalia"

Glencoe was a small town, and like all small towns it was devoted to gossip. I knew my classmates had heard about my father—many of them had probably even driven past Goodyear to see the broken window the way they'd drive past a body shop to see a car that had been totaled—but only Rob and a couple of other friends said anything. . . .

It took a couple of weeks for the gossip to reach me. One day during lunch Rob told me that Todd Knutson, whose father was a mechanic at Goodyear, was telling everybody my father had been fired for embezzling. "I know it's a dirty lie," Rob kept saying, "but some kids think he's telling the truth, so you'd better do something."

DAVID JAUSS

Checking Out the Checkout Line

standing in long lines can bring out the best and the worst in people (usually the worst). Because some people in the line are in a hurry—perhaps the dog or the baby is waiting in the car with the engine running—and because others are not in a hurry and would rather take their time sorting out their coupons, writing their checks, and then disputing the expiration date on the coupon to save a nickel on paper towels, this context is fraught with drama. Even with express lanes that limit purchases to nine or fewer items (ha!) and don't allow checks, as we all know, delays occur.

Given the emotional investment in checkout lines and the potential for conflicts, this is a context ripe for creative exploration. The following exercise asks you to invent a new approach to deal with this everyday hassle.

Panning Instructions

1. Invent a list of items passing on a checkout conveyor belt, mixing the typical with the bizarre: in a supermarket, for example, a loaf of bread, a can of peaches, a divorce decree, apples, a roll of paper towels, parsley, a ringing telephone, a nightstick, a headache, a half-gallon of milk, a bag of onions, a picture of Robert Redford, Robert Redford himself; or in a department store, leather gloves, baby bottles, a lit candle, a purse, a ringing telephone.
2. Linger by the cash register line in a supermarket, bookstore, drugstore, hardware store, or in any other kind of store, and observe and jot down the bizarre or unusual combinations people really do purchase—for example, in a grocery store, toilet paper, a single kiwi fruit, and a package of manila envelopes; in a hardware store, Christmas lights and rat poison, and so forth.
3. Begin a poem, story, or essay that incorporates your findings and imaginings from both lists.

Excavating Instructions

1. Write a piece in which you attempt to discover what a person's life is like from the real or imagined items placed on a checkout belt. Justin Cain begins to do this in "Get a Life," in which the protagonist reflects, apparently aloud, about a woman who buys a lot of cat food (see page 113). Allow your main character to pursue this speculation in a story, poem, or essay. Notice what purchases say about characters in John Updike's short story "A&P" (below).

2. Write a dialogue between two people in the checkout line that focuses totally on their purchases and the justification for them.

🕴 NUGGETS

From the short story "Get a Life"
The woman in front of me had placed maybe twenty-five cans of cat food on the conveyor belt—and for herself a carton of orange juice and a package of English muffins.

"Get a life," I heard myself saying without really wanting to say anything.

"I beg your pardon," the woman said.

I looked beyond her to the parking lot outside and said, "Oh, the kid out there on the motorcycle. I was talking to myself."

"No you weren't," she said. "You were talking to me. You think all this fuss over a cat is ridiculous, don't you?"

"Look, lady," I started to say, but then it hit me that this woman read my mind perfectly. It didn't make any sense to deny it.

JUSTIN CAIN

🐚 ARTIFACTS

From the short story "A&P"
Around they come, Queenie still leading the way, and holding a little gray jar in her hand. Slots Three through Seven are unmanned and I could see her wondering between Stokes and me, but Stokesie with his usual luck draws an old party in baggy gray pants who stumbles up with four giant cans of pineapple juice (what do these bums do with pineapple juice? I've often asked myself) so the girls come to me. Queenie puts down the jar and I take it into my fingers icy cold. Kingfish Fancy Herring Snacks in Pure Sour Cream: 49 cents. Now her hands are empty, not a ring or a bracelet, bare as God made them, and I wonder where the money's coming from. Still with that prim look she lifts a folded dollar bill out of the hollow at the center of her nubbled pink top. The jar went heavy in my hand. Really, I thought that was so cute.

JOHN UPDIKE

Exit Interview

ow often have you told only part of the truth during an interview? Perhaps you fudged the business about why you really left your last job, which wasn't *exactly* your idea but your manager's. Or maybe you stretched the truth just a bit when you told the college administrator that you were key to your high school French Club's success when, in fact, your main contribution was showing up for the yearbook picture.

Many of us are coached in the proper telling of these "white lies" by more experienced friends and relatives. We learn to turn questions around so we can answer them in ways that promote our strengths and detract from our weaknesses. For example, a good friend of ours who is famous for getting a job offer after each interview she's had, answers the inevitable question about her greatest weakness as an employee this way: "I need to learn to take breaks. I simply work too hard."

But what if we answered truthfully instead of making sure that we're seen in the most favorable light possible? While we might still be flipping hamburgers for the minimum wage at fifty or manning a lemonade stand at sixty, we'd be doing each with a completely clear conscience. The following exercises ask you to consider the creative possibilities that might arise if interviews were actually opportunities for self-reflection.

Panning Instructions

1. On a separate paper, answer the following ten "interview" questions as truthfully as possible:

> **1.** Tell me one thing about yourself so revelatory, personal, or embarrassing that I will never be able to look at you in the same way again.
>
> **2.** In what way are you secretly a "bad" person?
>
> **3.** What incident or decision in your past do you most regret routinely?
>
> **4.** What do you most regret about your childhood?
>
> **5.** What do you most regret about your adolescence?
>
> **6.** What do you most regret about your parents?
>
> **7.** What is the biggest lie you ever told? Why did you tell it?
>
> **8.** What one thing about yourself do you find completely revolting? Why?

9. Who do you wish you could have been born as? (Celebrities don't count here. Choose someone you know.) Why?

10. Why should you not be trusted?

2. Look over your answers, and circle or highlight in some way the ones that make you the most uncomfortable.

For example, one student answered number seven as follows: "I lied to my wife when I told her I'd never really been in love until I met her. In fact, I'm still in love half the time with Sharon, my first girlfriend." He answered number 10 as follows: "I can't be trusted because I can be flattered into doing almost anything."

Begin a poem, story, or essay that incorporates at least two of your answers, as in this continued example:

> My wife had no idea what a liar I was until the day Sharon showed up in our living room with her box of Avon products.
>
> "Wow, you still look great," she said to me when I walked in.
>
> I had just driven home on the freeway with an air-conditioning system in my car that was only working half-heartedly. My skin felt coated with a layer of grime and sweat, but with Sharon smiling at me, I felt the grime lift. She always had a way of making me feel better than I was.
>
> "You two know each other?" my wife asked, putting down a small spray bottle.
>
> "Once upon a time a very long time ago," Sharon said.
>
> "You haven't changed a bit," I said, instantly regretting how cliché that sounded. But she hadn't. Not really.

Feel free to fictionalize along the way.

Excavating Instructions

Many writers claim to know their characters so well that they could shop for them at a grocery, hardware, or clothing store and not have to return one item. Explore creating such a fully realized character by answering the questionnaire in the Panning Instructions for a person who is at least partially imagined (your character may initially be based on someone you know) whom you would like to work with in your writing.

Once again, circle the answers that make you the most uncomfortable, only this time you should be uncomfortable for your character, not yourself.

Begin another poem, story, or essay that incorporates in some way at least two of your new answers.

NUGGETS

From a short story in progress

As I walked up the steps to the warped porch of my parents' dark yellow house, I heard sounds of misdirected hate pour out of the small crack of the peeling front door. I knew my father had been drinking again. The indolent tone of his backsliding words reminded me of the other day when I had watched him down a pint of Smirnoff.

"Go take out the trash and wash those dirty dishes that you were supposed to wash this morning by the sink." My dad started yelling at me while my mom walked in a daze, wearing her pink knitted top, white slacks and white leather shoes that most dentist hygienists wear to work.

"Come back, Fynn. Don't leave." My mom screamed as she picked up a vase. I darted out of the house, slamming the door behind me. I heard something break against the door. It sounded like my mother's vase.

SEAN CHAFFINS

ARTIFACTS

From the short story "First Confession"

Nora was sitting on the railing, waiting for me, and she put on a very sour puss when she saw the priest with me. She was mad jealous because a priest had never come out of the church with her.

"Well," she asked coldly, after he left me, "what did he give you?"

"Three Hail Marys," I said.

"Three Hail Marys," she repeated incredulously. "You mustn't have told him anything."

"I told him everything," I said confidently.

"About Gran and all?"

"About Gran and all."

(All she wanted was to be able to go home and say I'd made a bad confession.)

"Did you tell him you went for me with the bread-knife?" she asked with a frown.

"I did to be sure."

"And he only gave you three Hail Marys?"

"That's all."

She slowly got down from the railing with a baffled air. Clearly, this was beyond her. As we mounted the steps back to the main road she looked at me suspiciously.

"What are you sucking?" she asked.

"Bullseyes."

"Was it the priest gave them to you?"

"'Twas."

"Lord God," she wailed bitterly, "some people have all the luck! 'Tis no advantage to anybody trying to be good. I might just as well be a sinner like you."

FRANK O'CONNOR

Modern Romance

S WM 6', 38, tall, intelligent, handsome, likes long walks on the beach, love songs, birdwatching ISO S/DWF slender, 30-38, good sense of humor, looking for life partner to share joys and sorrows. Please send note and picture to . . .

Sometimes modern romance begins with the personal ads. Typically, the ads describe handsome, successful people who long for romance and/or commitment. Adjectives such as *dynamic, slim, humorous, warm, good-looking, adventurous, youthful, sincere,* and *sensitive* abound.

It is not uncommon for ad writers to compare themselves to movie stars or even mythical figures. In a recent issue of the *Washingtonian,* an upscale magazine for those who live in the metropolitan District of Columbia area, one writer calls herself a Katherine Hepburn type while another describes himself as a White Knight.

While it makes sense that people are hesitant to admit their flaws when searching for love, it seems unlikely that this many dynamic, slim, humorous, warm, good-looking, adventurous, youthful, sincere, and sensitive people even exist.

⚡ Panning Instructions

1. Write a personal ad in which you describe all of your most unattractive qualities. Be as specific as possible and brutally honest, as Scott Patton is in "Or, You Could Bag It" (page 120). Celebrate your unique flaws and dislikes. (This ad may also be written in the form of a poem.) Some codes to help you get started:

- S = Single
- M = Married
- W = White
- B = Black
- J = Jewish
- D = Divorced
- ISO = In search of

2. Who would respond to your ad? Create a character who would be attracted to the "flawed" you, and have him or her write a letter back explaining why the two of you should meet for a date. Similar to the ad itself, this response may also be written in the form of a poem. For a creative nonfiction approach, describe the person you would like to answer your ad. What man or woman is worthy of falling in love with your true self?

3. With the advent of the Internet and e-mail, a whole new category of romance and romantic intrigue has evolved. In thousands of chat rooms and on thousands of electronic message boards, people of all ages express their views, give their impressions, display their wit, passions, dreams, and biases, and, increasingly, are finding sympathetic admirers and soul mates in cyberspace. However, as with personal ads, there is not always a correspondence between what a person is and what a person types on a keyboard. As an exercise, try producing a chat room dialogue between two people, each of whom is quite different from the person he or she represents in words. Use the outcome as a springboard for a story, poem, or essay.

Excavating Instructions

Re-examine the "flaws" you describe in your personal ad and begin a poem, story, or piece of creative nonfiction defending your flaws as unique character traits. The main character in Donna Rhinegold's story (below) chews her hair, a habit her boyfriend likes. Identify several bad habits and try answering the following questions to discover their singular value and meaning:

1. When did you begin _____ (cleaning your teeth with a credit card, chewing on your knuckle)?

2. If you stopped _____ (bouncing checks, sleeping with the TV on, and so on), would you still be you?

3. Who taught you how to _____ (slurp a soda, drink coffee out of a saucer)? What did that person mean to you?

NUGGETS

A start on a story

I began chewing my hair relatively late in life, during my second year in college, and I began doing it specifically when I was in doubt about the outcome of something rather imminent. I had grown increasingly doubtful about Dr. Krueshnik's ability to get through another lecture on inorganic chemistry since he appeared to have become so bored with the subject that he could hardly bring himself to pronounce the name of another reagent. This task was itself complicated by the fact that he was drunk now more often than not. Chewing the tips of my hair felt like the only thing I could do under the circumstances.

My mother noticed this habit when I came home over Christmas break, and she told me to stop many times. But I couldn't. It was so easy, my hair being right there, and there being so many things almost about to happen. Surprisingly, the boy who would become my boyfriend that year liked it that I chewed my hair. He thought it was sexy—but then he thought every nervous trait in a girl was sexy.

DONNA RHINEGOLD

 ## ARTIFACTS

From the article "Or, You Could Bag It"

. . . I toyed briefly—about six minutes—with the idea of answering one of those personal ads in another newspaper, but I am not a "nurturing, caring, long-walks-on-the-beach, reading poetry by the fire, Alan Alda-Judd Hirsch kind of guy." Nor am I looking for someone with "plenty of love" seeking an "immediate lifetime commitment" who's "poor but rich in friends." And is anyone really looking for a "leather-loving mistress who will make you obey"? I don't think so.

Nor am I about to place such an ad: "Divorced white guy, can't dance, smokes cigars, waist size and golf handicap match, prefers long evenings in front of the TV waiting to let the dog in, not willing to drive out of N. VA., even for dinner."

SCOTT PATTON

Half Accountant, Half Bartender

t's hard to find a character more hackneyed than the tough-as-nails-on-the-outside/heart-of-gold-on-the-inside prostitute. But what about a prostitute who takes cake decorating classes through Parks and Planning? Or a trash collector who sings opera in community theater? Now we have the beginnings of potentially interesting characters, that is people who are capable of surprising us.

Of course, no one is exactly who he appears to be. The man we pass on the street each day, who hurries past us in his tailored business suit, a cell phone ringing in his briefcase, may secretly wear under one shirt cuff a friendship bracelet his five-year-old daughter made for him or perhaps there is a rose tattooed on his ankle. The quiet librarian we count on always to direct us to the right stacks may race dirt bikes on weekends.

The problem is, we usually don't know much about the real lives of people we are used to seeing in only one role, so we stereotype. A business-woman is either brusque, or, like the tough-as-nails prostitute stereotype, maybe she's actually longing to give it all up for domestic bliss. What we might not imagine is a more complex truth: she likes her career just fine, thank you, but her life would be meaningless if she had to give up collecting tiny porcelain horses.

The following exercises ask you to begin creating truly complex characters by melding the characteristics generally associated with one character with those usually associated with another.

Panning Instructions

1. Mythology is rich with creatures that are half one thing, half another. The centaur has the body of a horse and the head of a man; the Minotaur, the head of a bull, the body of a man. Mermaids are blessed and cursed with being split down the middle: half-woman/half-fish. Create your own myth by blending two "types" of people you generally think of as having distinctly different characteristics. Begin your own **list** from scratch or add to the one we have begun below.

nurse
bodybuilder
swimmer
baker
runner
lawyer
teacher
nanny
rock climber
glass blower
flutist

2. After you have decided on the two types your characters will embody—for example, nanny/rock climber—decide on her physical characteristics. We imagine our nanny/rock climber wearing her hair in a tight English bun but sporting hiking shorts instead of a prim dress. *Draw a picture of your creation.*
3. When you finish either praising or laughing at your artwork, begin a story, poem, or essay in which this character figures centrally. If you have trouble getting started, have your "centaur" be misread by someone who notices only half of who he or she is.

Excavating Instructions

Perhaps we are strongly influenced by the way others look on the outside because we have so little to go on when we meet people. Certainly, though, it is a failure of our imaginations when we let physical impressions dominate. How would frogs ever be kissed into princes? Beasts turned into beauties?

For this exercise, choose from your original list, but this time create a character who is physically all one thing, but spiritually at least one other. For example, you might create a body builder with the soul of a harp player or, conversely, a harp player with the soul of a body builder. If it helps you get started on a new poem, story, or essay, you may wish to have your body builder take harp lessons (or your harp player find a trainer at the gym).

🜂 NUGGETS

From the story, "Half Lawyer, Half Skydiver"

Laura was going to vomit if one more person called her stable or boring. So she was a successful lawyer at the age of 25! That didn't mean she knew where she was going in life or that she didn't know how to have fun. The lawyer in her was more something her parents wanted her to be than Laura herself wanted to be. . . .

NIKOLE SLAGAL

From a story in progress

Esther despised the sucking sound of the pump, but it was the only thing that brought her mother relief from the repulsive build-up of bile in her stomach. For the last hour Esther had been watching her mother sleeping fitfully. She suspected the contortions were due to the three-foot-long tube stuck down her mother's nose.

What a lousy ending, Esther thought as she took off her blazer and folded it neatly across the only chair in the tiny room. She closed her eyes and rubbed the dangling silver symbol at her throat.

Never in a million years did Esther expect such a messy conclusion to her mother's blithe Sagittarian life. Sagittarians are known for their happy-go-lucky demeanor, for their slightly loopy, yet always charming way of handling almost any situation. A massive heart attack and instant death after a fierce orgasm would have been a far more fitting ending to her mother's life.

But instead, her mother's demise was more like the tragic Pisces. The constant pain, the useless surgery, the mysterious inflammation, the bevy of doctors, the confusion, the catheters, the deadly, aggressive tumor. Sarcoma.

DEBBY THOMPSON

ARTIFACTS

From "The Baboon Hour"

There was an aristocratic drawl in her voice that didn't jibe with the disturbing way Rachel Beale sat in a chair. The woman's blend of powder and cologne. I couldn't have said what it was at the time—not high-church exactly. There was something of an incongruity in her I'd not seen at such close range—good and bad ideas heaped up on one outfit. If her dresses were subtle, her jewelry was too bangly, too noisy. But somehow all that racket, her "sounding brass or tinkling cymbal," seemed manifestly honest to me; the weathered skin, which I'd associated with hard women, was clean and trustworthy. And no matter how much my mother protested, Rachel just did what she felt like doing and brought magazines.

BEVERLY COYLE

In the Gold Mine

The Elements

In most respects, the ancient world was much simpler than the modern world. In the ancient world, people recognized only four basic elements—earth, air, fire, and water—and these elements were considered not only the building blocks of the material world but also the elements of our characters and psyches. Thus, someone known to be passionate was thought to be possessed of fire and to be subject to the laws of fire. These earthly elements also had their correspondence in the heavens, and each astrological sign was—and still is—associated with earth (Capricorn, Taurus, Virgo), air (Gemini, Aquarius, Libra), fire (Leo, Sagittarius, Scorpio), or water (Pisces, Cancer, Aries).

Even though as moderns we must acknowledge the findings of science, the existence of more than 200 chemical elements, and the lack of empirical evidence connecting the affairs of people with the affairs of the stars, the language, imagery, and sense of wonder we associate with these concepts from the ancient world—with its alchemists and wizards—still capture our imaginations.

Try revisiting this simpler world by focusing on and using the ancient elements to organize a piece of fiction, a poem, or an essay.

Panning Instructions

Brainstorm a list of places where you would least expect to find each of the elements, as in the example below.

Fire
- In the refrigerator
- On the palm of my hand
- In a laundry basket
- In a piano

Make up a **list** of verbs that you would least associate with each element, as in the list below.

- The water sneezed
- The fire slept
- The wind stood in line

Combine the places in the first step with the verbs in the second, along with other more conventional material, and **freewrite** to see where it takes you. If you find yourself delighting in the language and rhythm and imagery of what you are writing, consider shaping your freewriting into a poem; if you find yourself inventing a plot, try writing a story; and if you find yourself exploring a personal situation in a fresh way, try beginning an essay.

Excavating Instructions

Begin a poem, story, or essay that expresses your relationship with parents, children, friends, and others using the **freewriting** you produced above. Feel free to mix up the elements as they suit your intentions, as Charles Jenkins does in his poem "Housefires and Homefries" (below).

NUGGETS

Housefires and Homefries

My mother sets little fires in my
shoes. They smolder like samovars.
It's her way of saying
stay home and wait for the glacier,
my father, man
of men. His golf bag is full
of snow. His shirts have ice cuffs
and frozen collars. My parents stare
at each other until their eyes turn
to earth and ash and when one speaks
the other blows air into paper bags
and the bags float like syllables
spoken under water.
They have filled their waterbed
with gasoline in anticipation
of making love and the obligatory
sharing of a cigarette.
I'm their little fireman who rushes in
with a garden hose
to douse them with marigolds.

CHARLES JENKINS

 ARTIFACTS

The Elements

We stay in motels named
after suspect gems,
The Topaz, The Blue Ember
because we love festive ideas
that failed or fell to ruin

and nothing is as festive or failed
as small swimming pools at night,
lit and empty.
We talk ourselves into silence
then slide into the water
and sink heavy
like unidentified corpses.

Cross-legged on the bottom,
our hair billowing up
like sea plants, we try
to say things with our hands
impossible in the air.
Our lungs ache for understanding
and the rule is
that only in understanding
may we rise.

But even here we try to speak.
The syllables leave our lips
silver and perfect and silent.
They rise, one after the other, and burst
on the mercurial sky.

Then we smile a chlorine smile
and return to our element, our room
in the Irish Diamond, The Rose
Quartz, the Sleepy Sapphire.

MICHAEL C. SMITH

Folk Remedies

Folk remedies for minor maladies abound in our culture, and they are often as odd as they are colorful, combining a little science with a lot of myth. Cures for the hiccups are perhaps among the oddest and most colorful. For hiccups, we tell the victims to hold their breath and count to ten or to drink a glass of water with a spoon in it. A more radical remedy involves scaring the person half to death. And one remedy that defies reason is to twirl several strands of hair in one ear. It remains to be seen whether any of these work, though those who offer such remedies swear by them.

The following exercises ask you to try your hand at inventing "folk"-sounding remedies for the hiccups or any other minor ailment (such as itching, charley horses, yawning, sneezing, ringing in the ears, warts, acne, bunions)—the odder the remedy the better. If you have inherited great folk remedies or discovered some of your own that really work, you may want to use these instead.

Panning Instructions

1. Invent two plausibly odd remedies for whichever ailment you wish to cure. For the first remedy, use the prompts provided. For the second, invent your own.

- To cure _____, place two _____ in a _____ and shake. Next stand on a _____ and drink the concoction while squeezing your _____ .
- To cure _____ do the following: _____ .

2. Begin a poem, story, or essay that incorporates one of these "cures."

Excavating Instructions

Problematic relationships and irritating behaviors have been dealt with using folk remedies just as baffling as those for physical ailments like hiccups and itching. Folk remedies abound for repairing a broken heart: go shopping, eat chocolate, get some sleep, travel. But how do you deal with the co-worker who continually whistles "Jingle Bells" while he works, even in July? How do you handle the man who can never meet you eye-to-eye but must cast his stare south? How do you fix the person who, despite your corrections, always gets your name wrong in exactly the same way—who calls you Janet when your name is Janice or Susan when your name is Suzanne?

For this exercise, develop in a poem, story, or essay a folk remedy for problematic relationships or irritating behaviors. To qualify as a folk remedy it should combine elements of common and uncommon sense. In Shirley Hickman's story "Joseph: A Man with a Mission" (below), the remedy provided by Aunt Nottie to ward off unwanted attention almost makes sense.

🕺 NUGGETS

From the short story "Joseph: A Man with a Mission"

According to my Aunt Nottie, if you wanted to get a man to stop looking at you, one sure way of doing it was to complain about your teeth. This, of course, would probably not work with a dentist, but then Joseph was not a dentist. So following her advice, I let it be known in the loudest way that my teeth were like toppling, unvisited gravestones.

In the break room one afternoon, there I was and there Joseph was, staring, ogling, preparing to begin to start to say something he concluded after long thought was clever but which would undoubtedly be insulting or just stupid. I bought a Snickers candy bar, took one bite and let out a shriek that probably woke up half the employees on the graveyard shift. Joseph looked genuinely startled.

"What's wrong?" he asked.

I palmed my jaw, winced and mumbled as though through swollen cheeks, "My tooth. I think I broke another one."

"Another one?"

"Yep, I don't have but maybe two good teeth in this head."

And then, wouldn't you know it, the fool smiled.

"And such a pretty head it is," he said.

I don't think my Aunt Nottie's wisdom grew out of a world with dental plans. Joseph seemed like a man prepared to see me through every root canal and bridge any dentist could build in my mouth. I needed another strategy.

SHIRLEY HICKMAN

From a start on a short story, "One Idea"

"To cure athlete's foot, place two pennies in a vodka tonic and shake. Next, stand on a catamaran and drink the concoction while squeezing your ankle."

This is the advice that my uncle gave me when I was twelve. I had never had athlete's foot before, but I hoped there was some other way to get rid of it. For one thing, I wasn't allowed to drink yet and for another, no one I knew had a catamaran. My uncle had a row boat that he called his yacht. He kept it in our backyard, and I don't know when the last time he took it out was. It was filled with rain water and leaves, which maybe was a good sign: if the rain didn't leak out there couldn't have been any holes in it. Not that I could ever imagine him actually carrying that boat down to the river that ran just outside of town. My uncle was more of a talker than a doer.

SEAN CARTER

ARTIFACTS

How to Cure Your Fever

Pull your bed aside and dig
a hole in the dirt floor.
Trick your wife, the one you divorced
a hundred years ago, so that
she falls asleep in this hole.
Replace as much dirt as possible.
Now drag the bed back
and center it over the spot.
As your fever subsides
think of the lawnmower in your heart,
try not to freeze.

THOMAS LUX

The Cliché's the Thing

t was a decent living. Even though I worked like a dog with my nose to the grindstone, I ate three square meals a day. Anyway, complaining wouldn't get me anywhere. I got up when the rooster crowed at the crack of dawn and went to bed when night fell. Weekends, I'd paint the town red. Sundays I'd put on my Sunday-go-to-meeting clothes and go to church . . .

If this passage fails to rivet your attention, it might be because it is full of phrases so familiar and overused that you no longer even hear them. At one time, perhaps, the expression "three square meals a day" seemed like a clever and snappy thing to say. Likewise, "nose to the grindstone" once probably evinced winces with its painful imagery. But because we have heard these expressions so often, we no longer really visualize the imagery they create. When a word, phrase, or gesture reaches this degree of familiarity, it's called a cliché.

If the creative can be characterized as fresh, surprising, and original, then clichés, in any realm—words, ideas, gestures—might be considered the opposite: stale, predictable, stock. Clichés have their place in our conversations, but resorting to them in creative writing can deaden or obscure the fresh things we're trying to say and give the impression of a lazy imagination.

Still, few writers can totally avoid clichés because clichés do have the power of lived truths, however familiar their expressions. An excellent and fun way of training the mind and ear to detect clichés is to embrace them and try to recast them in new ways and contexts—and in the process, perhaps, to discover some ideas for beginning poems, stories, or essays.

Panning Instructions

List as many clichés as you can. Mix and match key parts of several different clichés and try to come up with expressions that sound like clichés but are, in fact, new, as the late Weldon Kees does in the poem "Back" (page 135). Mixing and matching some of the clichés from the example given at the beginning of this exercise might result in something like the following:

I worked like a decent rooster.
Crowing wouldn't get me to Sunday.
I went to bed when night cracked.
I ate the red grindstone and painted three square dogs a day.

While largely nonsense, the above passage nevertheless sounds familiar, which makes the reader work for the sense it does make. In this way, modified clichés can forcefully direct the reader's attention.

Try your hand at writing a few lines of poetry or prose that use modified clichés. If you have trouble coming up with clichés—which, with respect to creative writing, would be a "good" failure—choose a few from the following list:

as old as the hills	*a tower of strength*
as a crow flies	*proud as a peacock*
one thing or another	*like a house on fire*
to beat the band	*sharp as a tack*
the whole nine yards	*smart as a whip*
lock, stock, and barrel	*gentle as a lamb*
everything but the kitchen sink	*hard as a rock*
till hell freezes over	*dead as a doornail*
fair to middlin'	*true to life*
nine-to-five job	*easy as pie*
almighty dollar	*as a matter of fact*
there but for the grace of God	*fair but firm*
excuse me for living	*bigger than life*
federal case	*around the clock*
to tell the truth	*a coon's age*
kicked the bucket	*rock bottom*
hightailed it out of here	*a slow death*
the bottom line	*raining cats and dogs*

Excavating Instructions

Write a poem, story, or essay that literalizes, engages, or challenges the truth expressed in a cliché.

To literalize a cliché, you simply take an expression, such as "kicked the bucket," which means to die, and make it actual or real—for example, "Yesterday, my dad kicked the bucket. He kicked it down the stairs. Kicked it into the yard. He was so angry, he kicked it into Mr. Simmons's ornamental cabbage garden."

To engage a cliché is to illustrate and use its truth. For example, "When my brother disputed his tax bill, he was in fact making a federal case out of it. He had no choice. And a federal case is different from other kinds of cases in ways that astonish even attorneys."

To challenge a cliché is to refute the common truth associated with it. For example, "No nine-to-five job is ever just nine-to-five . . . usually it's more like 7:30 to 6:30 by the time you add in driving and overtime . . . and that's my problem with the expression."

🜚 NUGGETS

Piety
Pull the wolf over her eyes:
Darkness is a trick
to a woman sacrificed.

Moss grows thick
on word and heart,
hiding forests from trees,

shading dawn from the sun.
Still, the Wolf of God
watches as she bleeds,

grins as she squints
through the hood
toward the moonlight.

He wants to crack her bones,
but his own skeleton
still isn't dry.

Pull the wolf over her eyes;
darkness is a trick
to a woman sacrificed.

PEGGY BAIR

 # ARTIFACTS

Back

Much cry and little wool
I have come back
As empty-handed as I went.

Although the woods are full,
And past the track
The heavy boughs are bent

Down to my knees with fruit
Ripe for a still life, I had meant
My trip as a search for stones.

But the beach was bare
Except for drying bones
Of a fish, shells, an old wool

Shirt, a rubber boot,
A strip of lemon rind.
They were not what I had in mind.

It was merely stones.
Well, the days are full.
This day at least is spent.

Much cry and little wool:
I have come back
As empty-handed as I went.

WELDON KEES

Crossing Relationship Boundaries

To identify a relationship is, to a certain degree, to circumscribe it. Friends, lovers, spouses, parents, children, brothers, sisters—all name relationships that have as many limits as rewards. We do things with our children we would not ordinarily do with our spouses or siblings, and vice versa. You might say that your father is your best friend, but would this really be a good relationship if it were true? We instinctively scrutinize mother/daughter relationships that get too much like friendships—the mother who flirts with her daughter's friends or who dresses a generation away from her own closet.

However, within limits, it might be said that the best relationships of any kind are those that threaten to cross boundaries, while nevertheless resisting for the good of all. The following assignment is designed to explore the boundaries of relationships and to play with them creatively.

Panning Instructions

Make up several lists that complete the following statement for different relationships:

Things I Do with My (fill in a relationship) That I Would Never Do with My (fill in a relationship).

Example: Things I Do with My Sister That I Would Never Do with My Best Friend

- Share shoes
- Hit each other over the head
- Lip sync to songs on the radio

Next, begin a poem, story, or essay in which you do some of the things that you say you would never do. In the beginning of an essay by Mark Lovell (page 137), a father reflects on an odd development in his relationship with his eight-year-old son.

☀ Excavating Instructions

Create or describe a relationship between two people in the act of redefining the boundaries of their relationship. For an example, see the excerpt from *A Home at the End of the World* (below), in which a mother smokes marijuana with her son and her son's friend. In Theodore Roethke's classic poem "Elegy for Jane" (below), a teacher questions his "right" to feel certain emotions about a student.

☀ NUGGETS

A beginning of an essay

I don't know when I started asking my son for advice. Sometimes it seems like decades ago, but I know that can't be right: he's only eight. . . . I seem to recall him telling me we should just go ahead and buy a new car after I'd complained to him about the difficulty of making payments on my salary. "Get a second job at night," he advised. Was he only five then?

MARK LOVELL

☀ ARTIFACTS

From the novel *A Home at the End of the World*

As I put the cigarette to my lips, I was aware of myself standing in a pale blue blouse and wraparound skirt in my son's bedroom, about to perform the first plainly illegal act of my life. I inhaled. The smoke was so harsh and bitter I nearly choked. My eyes teared, and I could not hold the smoke in my lungs as Bobby had told me to do. I immediately blew out a thick cloud that hung in the air, raggedly intact, for a full second before dissipating.

Nevertheless, the boys cheered. I handed the cigarette to Bobby.

"You did it," he said. "You did it."

MICHAEL CUNNINGHAM

From the poem "Elegy for Jane"
My Student, Thrown by a Horse

If only I could nudge you from this sleep,
My maimed darling, my skittery pigeon.
Over this damp grave I speak the words of my love:
I, with no rights in this matter,
Neither father nor lover.

THEODORE ROETHKE

What Things Say

Writing teachers often enjoin their students to "show, not tell," and in so doing they emphasize the imagination's dependence on and delight in images or words that appeal to the senses. It isn't that words that characterize or summarize or generalize—words such as *hate, love, ugly, smart, sad, stupid, playful, dangerous, horrible, good,* or *bad*—are in any absolute sense bad. Such words have their place. But often they simply aren't enough to convey a unique idea, or, at their worst, they tell the reader how to feel without giving her a chance to form her own impressions from events and other details.

Consider the following two statements about the same character:

1. The waiter left the check, and Harold calculated the tip based on a straight 15 percent, which came to $1.90. He called the waiter back and asked for change for a dollar, and he left all but the dime on the other dollar bill. He placed the dime in his change purse, a shiny red plastic device that opened like a wound.

2. Harold was cheap.

As a reader you may or may not agree with the wholesale conclusion that Harold was cheap, but we suspect that most readers would come away with something more from the first passage. Usually, readers would rather use their imaginations to discern the meanings of concrete details than to be told at the outset what things mean. When writers force their judgments, conclusions, or generalizations on readers without providing the details, the readers lose patience, as well they should.

Panning Instructions

1. Try your hand at replacing the following wholesale judgments with your own specific details (using words that appeal directly to the senses):

- She was an awkward conversationalist.
- The room smelled funny.
- He was a bad father.
- His car was a real jalopy.

2. Begin a story, poem, or essay that incorporates one of your developed descriptions.

Excavating Instructions

Because everyone is unique and because no one can know for sure what's going through another person's mind, people are by their very nature mysterious. Often, people don't even know themselves well enough to describe their own characters, so whether it's healthy or not, we look for and rely on clues about each other in trying to infer each other's needs, desires, and motives. It's as though we're all low-level sleuths: we observe how a friend suddenly turns down an offer of a beer, or how our boss begins to close his door after years of leaving it open, and we wonder what it all means. What can we infer from these details?

In a fashion similar to Weldon Kees's poem "Crime Club" (below), begin a story, essay, or poem by describing objects in a room that both raise questions about the inhabitant and also provide some answers. Notice how, after surveying his prospective dorm mate's possessions, Jonathan Francis suspects that his father followed him to college (below).

NUGGETS

From the essay "My New Roommate"

I had hoped to check into my dorm room before my assigned dorm mate, whoever that might be, so that I could tag the best bed. But I was too late. He had already been there. Moreover, judging from the objects my new roommate dumped in the room, whether or not I got the best bed would be the least of my worries. An issue of *Golf Life*? A rotary rack of tobacco pipes? A suitcase of unopened scotch and vodka bottles? Suddenly, I thought my dad had followed me to college and decided to move in with me.

JONATHAN FRANCIS

ARTIFACTS

Crime Club

No butler, no second maid, no blood upon the stair.
No eccentric aunt, no gardener, no family friend
Smiling among the bric-a-brac and murder.
Only a suburban house with the front door open

And a dog barking at a squirrel, and the cars
Passing. The corpse quite dead. The wife in Florida.

Consider the clues: the potato masher in a vase,
The torn photograph of a Wesleyan basketball team,
Scattered with check stubs in the hall;
The unsent fan letter to Shirley Temple,
The Hoover button on the lapel of the deceased,
The note: "To be killed this way is quite all right with me."

Small wonder that the case remains unsolved,
Or that the sleuth, Le Roux, is now incurably insane,
And sits alone in a white room in a white gown,
Screaming that all the world is mad, that clues
lead nowhere, or to walls so high their tops cannot be seen;
Screaming all day of war, screaming that nothing can be solved.

WELDON KEES

Changes in Preference

Most of us are creatures of habit. This is particularly true with matters of taste. Some people would rather reverse their position on capital punishment than reconsider their opinion of liverwurst. For every thousand people who change their party affiliations from Republican to Democrat, perhaps two will decide to give opera another chance. Significant change is inherently telling and dramatic.

The following exercises ask you to explore changes in preferences as potential sources of ideas for stories, poems, or essays. As you have been doing with the other exercises in this book, jump into these exercises uncritically and see where they take you. They may lead you into a scene or a character portrait or an entire short story—or you might discover some ideas better developed in an essay format.

Panning Instructions

Consider the history of one or two of your own preferences, and **freewrite** on the process you went through in establishing the preference, as nearly as you can remember. In this account, address some or all of the following questions:

- When did you start liking or hating some of the things you now like or hate?
- What was going on when you developed these preferences?
- Who was involved?
- Was there one incident that shaped your desire?

Excavating Instructions

Try accounting for one of your own changes of preference or inventing a situation that gives rise to a change of preference in a fictional character. Such changes are not always rational or carefully considered. As with the poem "A Bird a Boy and His Cups" (page 142), such changes sometimes appear to come from nowhere or from events that seem to have no relationship to the change.

NUGGETS

A Bird a Boy and His Cups

All afternoon I watched my son discover
and rediscover his red, blue
and yellow cups, each
a different size. It would be a month
before he stacked them right. For now
they were hard and bright
and they held each other sometimes.

On the deck rail a large starling
also watched. The bird cocked its head
approvingly, I would say, and seemed to reach
some judgments about the boy's promise.

Suddenly, I wanted to eat a fresh
lemon, a fruit whose flavor, I swear
to you, I never liked and have since
never ceased to like. If I were called

before the court of tongues
as a witness, I would still have little
to say for the lemon, only
that it is yellow and sour,
sometimes surprising,
but mainly yellow and sour.

FRANK SLAVINSKI

ARTIFACTS

From the short story "Juggling"

Wayne says of all the players involved, why should Joanne be the one Tyler blames. He says Tyler has to learn to look inside himself for answers and not to the outside world for fault. At Julia's house, Tyler's father made herb tea and asked Tyler to have a seat. Julia's at her aerobics class, Calvin said, otherwise she would be happy to meet you. Tyler had never seen his father drink anything warm. In the mornings he drank orange juice but never coffee. At night ice floated in his drinks.

SUZANNE GREENBERG

Subtitles and Doubletalk

ometimes what we say to people is not exactly what we mean—or *all* that we mean. We may politely tell a telemarketer trying to sell us credit card protection or vacation condos, "Thanks, but I'm not interested," when our actual thoughts say, "You total idiot! I'm so sick of these calls! Go jump in a lake." And when someone you really don't want to see, much less talk to, wants to get together for lunch, manners dictate that you uplift even as you let down by saying something like, "What a great idea. Maybe next week when things slow down at work a bit," while your thoughts are saying, "Give up a lunch hour to someone who never stops talking about herself? No way!"

These exercises ask you to take a closer look at conversations you have had in which you have sacrificed honesty for politeness or simply tried too hard to be "nice."

𐤀 Panning Instructions

Recall a situation in which you said one thing to someone—for example, your boss, a relative, or a friend—but felt or thought something entirely different. **Freewrite** about this for a while, recording what you said and thought and exploring why you didn't say what you thought. Next, write a segment of dialogue in which you include what you said as best as you can recall; then write what you were actually thinking in parentheses. (This may sound challenging, but in virtually every conversation we have, manners dictate things we leave out or say.) The following is an example of one student's dialogue:

Mother:	Honey, I've got something important to tell you.
Daughter:	Oh, yeah? (Oh, no. This doesn't sound good.)
Mother:	Chuck and I have finally decided to make it official.
Daughter:	Official? (Oh, God, I hope this isn't what it sounds like.)
Mother:	That's right. We're getting married. Tying the knot.
Daughter:	That's terrific, Mom. I'm so happy for you. (When can I throw up? I hope you don't expect me to participate in this farce.)

Mother:	And guess who I want to be my bridesmaid? What do you think, honey? I'd be so proud.
Daughter:	Of course, Mom. Thanks for asking me. (Thanks for putting me on the spot here. You just knew I couldn't say no.)
Mother:	Oh, I'm so excited. I know I must sound like a silly teenager, but I swear, honey, I feel like I'm eighteen all over again.
Daughter:	You don't sound silly at all. You just sound happy. (You sound like an idiot. Why does getting married reduce women's IQs this way?)

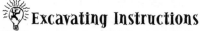 Excavating Instructions

Write a scene in which one of the speakers once again says one thing but means another. This time, allow your narration (the nondialogue part) to reveal the character's true feelings. You may wish to develop the scene you created for the **Panning Instructions** (as in "My Mother's Marriage" by Irene Cabel, below) or to invent an entirely new scene.

If you're working on an essay, recall a time when your words were less than honest. If you're working on fiction or poetry, invent a character and a scene, or change the facts of something that really happened.

NUGGETS

From the essay "My Mother's Marriage"

When my mother called to tell me that she was marrying Chuck, I said, "That's terrific, Mom. I'm so happy for you," although the truth was I didn't exactly feel like celebrating. My mother had been dating Chuck, a man who insisted on calling me "Renie" even though no one else did, and I hated it, for five years so it was hardly a surprise. Still, this was mother we were talking about, the woman who had married my father once upon a time and who now was planning to marry a man who made Andy Griffith seem like a big-city sophisticate.

"And guess who I want to be my bridesmaid?" she said next. "What do you think, honey? I'd be so proud."

I could just see her examining her manicure at the other end of the line while she waited for me to answer. My mother was small and Southern and always well-groomed. Me, I was five-foot-ten by the time I was fourteen and had to buy my size-eleven shoes from a catalog if I wanted any kind of selection. The only thing we had in common was my dad, who gave her me, gave me my ungainly size, and then left us both. Still, she was my mother and I felt I had an obligation not to ruin her happiness.

"Of course, Mom. Thanks for asking me," was all I said.

IRENE CABEL

ARTIFACTS

From the short story "A Good Bet"

Ada picks up the phone when Phil calls to check in. She would like to tell him the truth, that his daughter is sullen and lacks the ability to concentrate. But Phil already has enough problems. "We went to the movies tonight," Ada lies. "Something with John Wayne in it. Something about the west."

This seems to satisfy Phil. Ada can tell because he is quiet after she says it.

"She's a good girl," Ada says.

"That's good," Phil says. "John Wayne is good."

When Phil hangs up, Ada is alone with her heart again. But her heart is quiet. She takes the stethoscope that she stole from her doctor out of her night drawer and listens to the pounding, the everydayness of it, until she falls asleep.

SUZANNE GREENBERG

Setting as Character

An often unheralded element of stories, poems, and essays, setting—the physical context in which characters and actions are developed—can sometimes take on a life of its own. Who can forget the shower in Alfred Hitchcock's *Psycho* or the jungle in Joseph Conrad's "Heart of Darkness"? Whether minimal or richly detailed, setting always enters into how we imagine scenes, and to a certain extent, it can provide important clues to why characters behave as they do.

The following exercises ask you to focus on setting as a way of beginning stories, poems, or essays.

Panning Instructions

1. Fill in the blanks in the following sequence:

The room was _____ with six menacing-looking _____. He nearly bumped into a _____ that sat right in front of the _____, as though it were a _____ When he first entered the room he thought it was silent, but just as his eyes got used to the light, his ears began to detect a _____. Something about the _____ reminded him of his _____. Suddenly it came to him: he had entered his _____.

2. Use metaphors related to one of the items in List 1 to describe all of the items in List 2. Use the results to begin or develop a story, poem, or essay.

List 1
food
beds
carnivals
hunting
religion
weather
science

List 2
bed
lamp
chair
window
sofa
rug
illumination
odor
door
floor

Example using "weather":
"The carpet lay like a dark cloud over a vast floor. The heat in this room was oppressive as was the humidity. Steam seemed to radiate from the fat sofa. Five thin jagged lamps lit the room with a light almost too bright to see by."

Excavating Instructions

Try to recall a place from your childhood that affected you in some way. It might have been an apartment you lived in that faced a candy store or toy store—or a butcher shop or funeral home. Or perhaps it was a playground or fishing hole. **Freewrite** for ten minutes about the place, or simply list aspects of this place as you remember them. Don't worry about accuracy. All distant memories are to some extent created. If you get stuck, try organizing your reflections into descriptions, impressions, and feelings, including material for each. Continue to generate material until you feel compelled to introduce a character, perhaps yourself, at which point you will likely have a sense of whether a story, poem, or essay wants to be written. Notice how the excerpt from Robert Penn Warren's poem "Rattlesnake Country" in Artifacts (page 148) describes a house in the desert with extraordinary dramatic intensity. While the description contains several details, there is more here than a static landscape or scene: the "stonework" is *held* in place; the mesquite is "wolf-waiting"; the wicker chairs *follow* the "shimmering shade." This description conveys the sense that nature is about to collapse onto the house and reclaim the "little patch of cool lawn." This is rattlesnake country, and while a rattlesnake has yet to appear in the poem, the many alliterated *s* sounds—"shimmering shade," "sadly seeking," "shadow on a sun dial," "sprinkler ejects its misty rainbow"—provide an onomatopoetic suggestion of their presence. How would a character react to this setting?

☝ NUGGETS

From "A Day of Letting Go," a short story in progress

Their last date, he decided, would be at The Aquarium. It wasn't the best place to end a relationship, but at least they wouldn't be alone—he knew he wouldn't be able to pull it off if he were alone with her—and yet it wasn't too public, particularly on a week day.

He waited until they had entered the underwater observation cave featuring the seals. There was a nice stone bench facing the large windows behind which seals would occasionally swim by, rubbing their bellies against the glass. The cave was a little cold, which was appropriate, he supposed. It wasn't a warm message he had to deliver. The marine green light emanating from the windows was both festive in the way motel swimming pools are festive and yet eerie in the way a TV between active channels is eerie.

They sat for a while watching the seals parade sleekly. Predictably, Jeanette oo'd and ah'd, and the more she did it the more he was certain this relationship had to end. He had begun to hate seals, hate aquariums, hate wetness. The moment came, and he turned to her poised to do the deed:

"My god," she shouted suddenly, as though she had read his mind. But in fact she was pointing at the window where a seal with a large fish in its mouth swam by, the blood streaming copiously around them.

FERNANDO CRUZ

☝ ARTIFACTS

from "Rattlesnake Country"

Arid that country and high, anger of sun on the mountains,
    but
One little patch of cool lawn:
    Trucks
Had brought in rich loam. Stonework
Held it in place like a shelf, at one side backed
By the length of the house porch, at one end
By rock-fall. Above that, the mesquite, wolf-waiting. Its turn
Will, again, come.
Meanwhile, wicker chairs, all day,
Follow the shimmering shade of the lone cottonwood, the way
    that
Time, sadly seeking to know its own nature, follows
The shadow on a sun-dial. All day,
The sprinkler ejects its misty rainbow.

ROBERT PENN WARREN

Comparing Apples and Orangutans

Those of us who are fond of using comparisons and analogies in our quest to win arguments are often counseled not to compare two things, people, or situations that are too different to compare. When V says to Y that excessive shoe shopping is the same thing as excessive watching of football games, V can be expected to be scolded with, "You're comparing apples with oranges." While logic and rhetorical soundness may dictate that we mind our apples and oranges in argument, there are no such restrictions when it comes to creative writing. Indeed, the following exercises advocate comparisons that logic cannot digest.

Panning Instructions

1. Choose one or two of the following pairs of items and **freewrite** or **list** ways in which the two are similar. Use the result to begin a poem, story, or short essay.

> *a shirt and a chair*
> *birthdays and a catfish*
> *I Love Lucy (the television program) and spaghetti*
> *lightning and liverwurst*
> *justice and lava lamps*
> *swimming and voting*

2. Describe a person, real or fictional, by comparing the person implicitly to one of the fifty states. (An implicit comparison omits mention of the thing used in the comparison.) For example, you might compare your father to Nevada because he takes risks or gambles and he has a dry sense of humor. Use this as the basis of a poem, story, or essay.

Excavating Instructions

One of the delights of writing is discovering significant—though unlikely—connections between two things, people, or concepts hitherto unrecorded or unnoticed. For example, in the course of trying to describe a favorite aunt, you say that her voice was like the sound of a harp and suddenly you are off and running with not only the angelic associations related to harps but with the fact that harps are embraced in ways other musical instruments are not, a realization that illuminates both your relationship with your aunt and your understanding of harp music.

While such discoveries are often intuitive or inspired, try your hand at capturing the essence of someone you know by choosing a particular item in the following general categories and developing the comparison in two parts: first, say how the person is like the thing you chose and then say how the thing you chose is like the person. Finally, use these comparisons in a poem, story, or essay.

Category
Mammal
Fish
Bird
Insect
Flower
Tool
Musical Instrument
Dwelling
Structure
Institution
Sport
Religion

ꙮ NUGGETS

From the story in progress "Three and A Half Uncles"

Uncle Jasper had been divorced many years and never remarried. He had no kids, few friends, but he never seemed lonely. He was my dad's oldest brother, and my dad said Jasper was talented at keeping himself entertained. I never quite understood that, but I wondered if it had anything to do with the sense I often had that there was always someone with Jasper. Not just one person, but many. When he came to Christmas dinners, it was like a rugby team had elbowed open the front door bent on capturing the dining room—or whatever it is rugby teams do. In truth, I know nothing about rugby—maybe I saw a picture of a rugby team somewhere—a group of grown men advancing with a ball, muddy and sweaty. That was Jasper, both his physical gestures and his conversation.

RALPH MARGOLIS

 **ARTIFACTS**

The Life Beside This One

In the life you lead
Beside this one,
It is natural for you
To resemble America.
You require one woman.
You give her your name.

You work, you love;
You take satisfaction.
You are the president of something.
You are the same.

The children are clean,
They turn into lawyers.
They write long letters
And come home for Christmas.

It is a kind of Connecticut
Not to be twenty-five again.
Carefully in the evening
You do not think
Of the life you lead
Beside this one.

JOHN MORRIS

Citizen Oz

ovie lovers love nothing more than to compare, rate, and argue about the merits—artistic or otherwise—of their favorite movies. Every year, a list of someone's idea of the best movies appears in one publication or another, and periodically the results of polls taking in the whole history of cinema appear. For example, the following is a list of the 50 best films of the last century according to the American Film Institute and 1,500 other film experts:

1. *Citizen Kane*
2. *Casablanca*
3. *The Godfather*
4. *Gone with the Wind*
5. *Lawrence of Arabia*
6. *The Wizard of Oz*
7. *The Graduate*
8. *On the Waterfront*
9. *Schindler's List*
10. *Singin' in the Rain*
11. *It's a Wonderful Life*
12. *Sunset Boulevard*
13. *The Bridge on the River Kwai*
14. *Some Like It Hot*
15. *Star Wars*
16. *All About Eve*
17. *The African Queen*
18. *Psycho*
19. *Chinatown*
20. *One Flew Over the Cuckoo's Nest*
21. *The Grapes of Wrath*
22. *2001: A Space Odyssey*
23. *The Maltese Falcon*
24. *Raging Bull*
25. *E.T. The Extra-Terrestrial*
26. *Dr. Strangelove*

27. *Bonnie and Clyde*
28. *Apocalypse Now*
29. *Mr. Smith Goes to Washington*
30. *Treasure of the Sierra Madre*
31. *Annie Hall*
32. *The Godfather Part II*
33. *High Noon*
34. *To Kill a Mockingbird*
35. *It Happened One Night*
36. *Midnight Cowboy*
37. *The Best Years of Our Lives*
38. *Double Indemnity*
39. *Doctor Zhivago*
40. *North by Northwest*
41. *West Side Story*
42. *Rear Window*
43. *King Kong*
44. *The Birth of a Nation*
45. *A Streetcar Named Desire*
46. *A Clockwork Orange*
47. *Taxi Driver*
48. *Jaws*
49. *Snow White and the Seven Dwarfs*
50. *Butch Cassidy and the Sundance Kid*

Look over this list and circle five or ten movies that you have seen. Use these in the following exercises to generate poems, stories, and essays that draw from the best of the best. Or, if you prefer, draw ideas from other movies that speak to you.

⅄ Panning Instructions

1. Combine plot elements from two or three of these movies into a poem, story, or essay. For example, the plot of *Dr. Strangelove* involves preventing an accidental atom bomb attack and the plot of *The Wizard of Oz,* as most of us know, follows a little girl through a dream wherein she finds herself in a strange land and has several adventures as she tries to get home, aided by a scarecrow, a tin man, and a lion. Combining these plot elements might result in a story, poem, or essay that included a character trying to alert people to an imminent nuclear threat only he knows about. He could try to get in to see the president (*The Wizard of Oz*) but get turned away and meet several strange characters in his quest. An essay combining these two films might address the unreality of the nuclear age.

2. Choose one main character from two of the films from the list above and bring them together in a poem, story, or essay, for example, Sam Spade from *The Maltese Falcon* and the Von Trapp children from *The Sound of Music;* or Charles Foster Kane from *Citizen Kane* and McMurtry, the tragically sane character in *One Flew Over the Cuckoo's Nest.*

Excavating Instructions

Choose a movie that, in one way or another, had a significant impact on you and launch a story, poem, or essay that integrates elements from the movie with your life. Consider using the third-person point of view. For example, suppose that when you saw *Apocalypse Now,* the surrealistic blending of Conrad's "Heart of Darkness" and the Vietnam War, you began to see your own life as a jungle river from whose banks anything was likely to spring.

NUGGETS

From an essay in progress, "At Sea"

I often wonder what the deranged, ball-bearing-clicking Captain Queeg in *The Caine Mutiny* would have to say to Gilligan, the sailor on the TV series "Gilligan's Island." I wonder that perhaps because those extremes between crazed maniacal darkness and unbearable comic lightness seem too much like the skippers of my days. Consider: yesterday I discovered that my bank balance sank below zero, down into the Davey Jones's Locker of overdraft. I discovered this the hard way: the restaurant where I had breakfast, the quesadilla/chorizo special, with a side of flour tortillas, denied approval of my debit card. The manager was called. Other authorities were called. Conferences were held as to what to do with me. People looked at me in that way we look at people who wear too many shirts and pants. I just kept looking at that little bit of tortilla I didn't eat. I wanted it now, wanted it more than Queeg wanted command of his ship back. But I acted like Gilligan, all sheepish grins and pointed shoulders. But which one, I wondered, drove me onto the shoals of disrepute, the bulkhead ruptured, the masts splintered?

DONALD MCANDREWS

 ## ARTIFACTS

From "Steps"

How funny you are today New York
like Ginger Rogers in *Swingtime*
and St. Bridget's steeple leaning a little to the left

here I have just jumped out of a bed full of V-days
(I got tired of D-days) and blue you there still
accepts me foolish and free
all I want is a room up there
and you in it
and even the traffic halt so thick is a way
for people to rub up against each other
and when their surgical appliances lock
they stay together
for the rest of the day (what a day)
I go by to check a slide and I say
that painting's not so blue

where's Lana Turner
she's out eating
and Garbo's backstage at the Met
everyone's taking their coat off
so they can show a rib-cage to the rib-watchers
and the park's full of dancers with their tights and shoes
in little bags
who are often mistaken for worker-outers at the West Side Y
why not
the Pittsburgh Pirates shout because they won
and in a sense we're all winning
we're alive

FRANK O'HARA

He Said, Winkingly

When a mother calls her son by all three of his names—for example, John William Hanover—you can be fairly certain he's in trouble. And if she calls him by all three of his names after hanging up the phone with the principal at his elementary school, where he's famous for terrorizing kindergartners by telling them their teacher has a secret dungeon where she keeps kids after school, you can even guess at the tone of voice the mother might use when she says it. Maybe you even feel a little afraid for John William Hanover when you hear what she says next—"Get in here"—which, in its succinctness, carries more impact than a more elaborate "Get in here now, young man!" might carry.

We live in a world of dialogue, so we are expert at reading nuances into seemingly benign phrases and at uttering equally beguiling phrases ourselves. An exhausted mother may thrust her young baby at her husband when he comes home late from work and say, "Meet your father." The father hears this short sentence loaded with its implicit meanings: "I'm tired and beginning to feel bitter. You're never here. Why aren't you ever here? Thank God you're here. This baby doesn't even know who you are. Take over now because I desperately need a break."

And when the father takes the baby, holds her out in front of him, and says, "Is that a new boo-boo on your nose?" the mother hears: "You aren't taking good care of this baby. How did you let our child fall down? I can't even trust you to keep her physically safe while I'm gone." She also notices, although maybe not quite consciously, that her husband is speaking to the baby instead of to her. In fact, neither of them has spoken directly to the other yet. Instead, they're using the baby as go-between, a role she may resent in future years.

Too much reading into a simple exchange, you say? Maybe so, but learning to write and read dialogue can be part of the great joy of writing. The following exercises ask you to create rich, layered dialogue of your own.

Panning Instructions

1. The following phrases end with the kind of "tag lines" that beginning writers often rely upon to do the work that their dialogue should be doing on its own. For each of the five statements below, delete the tag line and include in its place a particular action that *shows* how the statement might have been uttered, as in the following example:

"I quit," he said, with uncertainty.
"I quit," he said. He stood up and walked toward the door but turned around when he got to it.

1. "I miss my sister," she said sadly.
2. "You make me laugh," she said in all seriousness.
3. "It was nice meeting you," he said, smirking.
4. "It's my turn to make the popcorn," she said angrily.
5. "Great movie pick," he said ironically.

2. Now that you have begun to set a scene and a mood by adding an action to a piece of dialogue, continue to develop this start by writing a line of response dialogue, followed once again by a brief action that illustrates how this might have been said. Consider creating an exchange that potentially means more than might initially appear to be the case, as in the example below.

"I quit," he said. He stood up and walked toward the door but turned around when he got to it.
"Did you forget something?" his ex-boss asked, already scribbling away in his appointment book.

3. Begin a poem, story, or essay with your exchange. If you choose to begin a poem, you might consider experimenting with line breaks and wording as in this example:

"I quit" he said and stood
and walked toward
the door but turned
when he got there
"did you forget some-
thing"(what you planned
to do next, where
your heart lives) his ex-boss
said, scribbling away already
in his appointment book

☀ Excavating Instructions

We all know families, and perhaps we even grew up in one, that shout their feelings at each other: "I hate you!" "You make me sick!" "Why did I ever marry you?!" However, once we pass through adolescence, most of us develop a bit more tact. "I hate you!" becomes "Why am I always the one taking out the garbage around here?" "You make me sick" is replaced with "We need to discuss our budget." "Why did I ever marry you?" becomes "Do you need me to show you how to use the dishwasher?"

Perhaps in no other area of creative writing is the maxim "less is more" more fitting than it is in dialogue. One exclamation point on a page makes the whole page scream with anger or excitement. One quiet "I'm leaving now" can dissolve an entire relationship.

Begin a poem, story, or essay that incorporates dialogue that talks around a major issue in a serious relationship between two people (father/daughter, spouses, best friends, and so on). Have the two avoid stating their feelings directly *and* responding to each other directly. In other words, have them respond in non sequiturs, which is, in fact, the way many of us speak, as in the example below.

> "I guess I'll be going now," I said. I adjusted the shoulder pads in my dark blue suit jacket.
>
> "Too bad you're not interviewing for a job as a flight attendant," my mother said.

☀ NUGGETS

From the novel in progress *Looped*

Elana makes her short, stubby legs go slack, defeating Sophia's attempts to stuff them into navy-blue tights. "Daddy doesn't do it that way," she pouts.

"Don't whine. You know Mommy doesn't like it when you're passive-aggressive."

Jonathan is looking over his raised chin to knot the sober paisley tie Sophia bought him for Christmas. "The driver will be out front in ten minutes. Are we picking your father up?"

"No, he'll meet us there. I didn't want to be locked into driving him around after." Sophia throws the tights on the bed. "How would you like to wear your snow suit to church?"

"Let me try, honey." Jonathan takes the tights and rolls them down to the feet. "Come on, buttercup, let's get all dressed up nice for grandpa."

Elana flops back on the bed and lets herself be dressed. Jonathan tucks her feet into the nylon toes and then tugs the tights up her legs. Then he buckles on her patent leather shoes. The doorbell rings. Elana springs from bed and runs shouting, "Gampa gampa gampa!"

Sophia stands with her arms crossed.

Jonathan says, "It isn't a contest."

"Thanks for the bulletin. She was supposed to wear the blue shoes with that dress."

ANDREW WINSTON

ARTIFACTS

From the short story "Horatio's Trick"

"How old is Melissa?" Charlotte asked.

"Twelve or thirteen," he said.

"Does she look like her mother?"

"Not much," Nicholas said. "But she's really her sister's kid, and I never saw her sister."

"Her sister's child?" Charlotte took a sip of her tea, which was laced with bourbon. She held it in her mouth a second before swallowing.

"Melissa's mother killed herself when Melissa was just a baby. I guess her father didn't want her. Anyway, he gave her up."

"Her sister killed herself?" Charlotte said. She could feel her eyes widening. Suddenly she remembered the night before, the open window in the bathroom, the black sky, wind smacking her in the face.

"Awful, huh?" Nicholas said, lifting the tea bag out of the mug and lowering it to the saucer. "Hey, did I shock you? How come you didn't know that? I thought you were the one with a sense for disaster."

ANN BEATTIE

Character by Association

When describing people, many of us look for the one perfect word that says it all. "The problem with my roommate is he's a real neat freak." "My first wife was a total bookworm." But while it can be satisfying to sum up others this way, these brief descriptions are almost always too limited to do complex beings justice. While a neat freak may spend an excessive amount of time straightening up and a bookworm an unusual amount of time reading, certainly these descriptions do not take into account entire characters.

In the following exercise, we ask you to explore new ways of discovering and describing character that should encourage you to look at real and/or fictional people in a way that does justice to the complexity of humankind.

Panning Instructions

1. Think about a person you know fairly well—a friend, relative, or coworker—whom you would like to write about for whatever reason. Then answer the following questions with respect to this person. Or begin to invent a character by answering the following questions:

If this person were a _____, what _____ would he or she be?

- Animal
- Flower
- Tree
- Color
- Food
- Country
- Model of car
- Kitchen utensil
- Odor
- Playing card
- Month
- Radio station

- Body of water
- Brand of soap
- Piece of jewelry

2. Begin a story, poem, or essay that incorporates one or more of the connections you have made above. Notice the way Judy Grahn compares Ella to a copperhead snake and later to an "isolated lake" in her poem "Ella, in a square apron, along Highway 80" (page 162). We included three associations that Kevin Harris used to develop "Howard" (see below). The animal that came to mind when Kevin thought about Howard was a giraffe, which suggested risk taking. To others, a giraffe might suggest gentleness.

Excavating Instructions

Instead of describing your character as one or more of the items listed above, link him or her to one of the things or places you have listed in a way that indirectly describes her personality. For example, in the excerpt from the short story "How Far She Went," notice the way an Impala—a large, rugged practical car—is really an extension of a particular woman who, in a rage, is "driven" to her actions. In Trey Hunigan's essay (below), a father is so closely associated with gadgets that a Dustbuster seems almost like another arm.

NUGGETS

From a story in progress, "Howard"
animal = giraffe
kitchen utensil = corkscrew
color = brushed gold

Howard could stick his neck out like no one else I knew. He sometimes took risks for the sake of taking risks. But often what looked to everyone else like a foolish risk would end up being a sound investment. Not glittery, but subtle, like brushed gold. Howard was like that, a class act, except for his reasoning, which was circuitous at best and downright screwy most of the time.

KEVIN HARRIS

From the essay "My Father the Dust Buster"
I used to think my father loved his gadgets more than he loved me. Or at least as much. He sold life insurance for a living, which seemed an abstract, sad

profession to me, and when I got older, I began to realize that it was more that he appreciated the solidness and realness of things than that he actually loved them. And nothing was realer to my dad than a new gadget.

After all, like all humans, my mother and I were composed of mostly water, and no one knew more than he, an insurance salesman, how quickly a life could be flushed out of a person. But a gadget was something else altogether, infinitely fixable, ready to take on the lowliest household task with an electric buzz of glee.

I remember my father and his first Dustbuster waking me early one Saturday morning, as smiling and open mouthed, both of them inched their way around my headboard.

TREY HUNIGAN

ARTIFACTS

Ella, in a square apron, along Highway 80
She's a copperheaded waitress,
tired and sharp-worded, she hides
her bad brown tooth behind a wicked
smile, and flicks her ass
out of habit, to fend off the pass
that passes for affection.
She keeps her mind the way men
keep a knife—keen to strip the game
down to her size. She has a thin spine,
swallows her eggs cold, and tells lies.
She slaps a wet rag at the truck drivers
if they should complain. She understands
the necessity for pain, turns away
the smaller tips, out of pride, and
keeps a flask under the counter. Once,
she shot a lover who misused her child.
Before she got out of jail, the courts had pounced
and given the child away. Like some isolated lake,
her flat blue eyes take care of their own stark
bottoms. Her hands are nervous, curled, ready
to scrape.
The common woman is as common as a rattlesnake.

JUDY GRAHN

From the short story "How Far She Went"

Furious, she ran to her car, past the barking dog, this time leaving him behind, driving after them, horn blowing nonstop, to get back what was not theirs. She drove after them knowing what they did not know, that all roads beyond that point dead-ended. She surprised them, swinging the Impala across their path, cutting them off; let them hit it!

MARY HOOD

"My Mother Was Like an Ornate Castle"

F ew topics engage the imagination of writers as much as relationships. Rarely simple, relationships with family, friends, and lovers bring out the best and worst in all of us. We run from relationships and we work at relationships. Some of us take our relationships with us into therapy. Even for those who lead relatively isolated lives, past relationships can be a powerful, life-defining force—sometimes defining enough to send us into hiding.

We write books and essays about relationships and feature them in sitcoms and epic tragedies: Romeo and Juliet, Oedipus and Creon, Cain and Abel, Burt and Loni, Julia and Lyle, Bruce and Demi. Comic, tragic, romantic, existential; light, heavy, murderous, meaningless. Relationships are what we are doing when we're not working or recovering from work.

The following exercises prompt you to explore relationships by comparing them to other things and processes and to muse on relationships that never happened.

Panning Instructions

1. Fill in the following blanks with specific relationships—real or imagined—and with *unexpected* similes (using *like* or *as* to join two different things). For example: My relationship with *my mother* was like *an ornate castle.*

- My relationship with _____ is/was like
  _____ .
- My relationship with _____ is/was like
  _____ .
- My relationship with _____ is/was like
  _____ .

2. Using one of the similes you have just created as a springboard or focus, **freewrite** or **free associate** reasons, justifications, or explanations for this comparison. For example: *My relationship with my mother was like an ornate castle because it was full of hidden passages and royalty.*

3. Now begin a poem, story, or essay using the material you generated. Notice how Janeen Miller's excerpt (below) would probably lead to a poem because of the imagery she uses.

Excavating Instructions

Some of our most romantic musings center on relationships that, for whatever reason, didn't materialize. Someone might find herself occasionally wondering how her life might have turned out differently if she had dated that person she could never even work up her nerve to speak to. Someone else might wonder what kind of relationship he would have had with his mother, who died when he was only two.

Begin an essay, story, or poem that explores either a real or fictional relationship that never happened but might have changed everything if it had.

NUGGETS

Lover's Canvas

A painting layered over to cover mistakes
the rough brush strokes so much paint spent
wasted in the effort turpentine couldn't even
dissolve it all the way
we did this one thing together right
the laying it on
the thick way we tried to cover up the past and
paint it over ending up with
the canvas of our relationship
one ruined city after another

MARIAM ROMELLO

From the **Panning Instructions**

My relationship with my mother is like the weather on an early spring day. It begins with the promise of freshness, warmth, renewal. With confidence I put on the shorts and T-shirt that were long hidden in the bottom of a drawer and rush outside.

For the first time in months, the sun feels warm on my skin. The birds sing their excitement. The sky is azure blue. I begin to trust that spring is really here. . . .

Puffy white clouds slowly build in the west. First one or two, then just as quickly, a dozen. I ignore them. By noon they darken and cover the sky. A cool breeze rises. I tell myself it will pass quickly. I want to trust this day.

By mid-day I can no longer deny the change.

JANEEN MILLER

ARTIFACTS

From the essay "Somewhere in the Eighties"

One day, during a quiet moment in what was to prove our last visit together before her death, my grandmother looked up from her coffee and spoke of her son, breaking a virtual silence of decades in so simple a manner that I knew she'd been asking the question of herself for thirty-some years. "I suppose you've often wondered," she said, "what would have happened if your father had been the one to live, if he'd been the one to raise you. . . ."

The only formal photograph of my family that I have ever seen was taken on Easter, 1953. My father, hair already whitening, is holding me; my mother stands beside him; my two sisters stand in front, and my yet-unborn brother is indicated only by the curve of my mother's coat. As I study this image, and think of the funeral that will take place five months later, I am still unable to wonder much about what might have been.

COLETTE BROOKS

As Restless as Pantyhose

Whether we are describing feelings, places, or people, most of us have a natural tendency to compare. "I was as scared as I was when I got caught at the beach during that hurricane." "She pleaded like a hungry child." We compare to describe and make sense of the world. If one thing is "like" something else, then nothing can be too peculiar or unusual to comprehend.

While comparisons can help us understand and explain, they can also limit our vision. Overreliance upon likely comparisons—similes—can cause us to circumscribe, or draw a careful border around, our world. We all know a person who, upon tasting anything unusual for the first time, declares it "tastes just like chicken" or who seems incapable of traveling anywhere without comparing the new places to his hometown.

In these exercises, you will experiment with making comparisons that will surprise you and increase your ability to make the kind of fresh connections that enrich writing.

Panning Instructions

1. The following is a list of adjectives set up to be turned into similes (comparisons using *like* or *as*). Quickly complete each (in a couple of different ways, if you wish), without worrying too much whether your comparisons are original.

As orange as	Stumbling like a
As empty as	Running like a
As hungry as	Crying like a
As blue as	Laughing like a
As dull as	Smiling like a
As fragile as	Gathered together like a
As arrogant as	Singing like a
As rough as	Trembling like a
As regular as	Praying like a
As tentative as	Grinning like a
As pliant as	Sailing like a

As terrified as	Suffering like a
As eloquent as	Coughing like a
As reliable as	Stinking like a
As restless as	Mumbling like a
As confining as	Screaming like a
As pale as	Bowing like a
As sweet as	Flirting like a

2. Next, mix and match the adjectives and nouns, looking for interesting results as in the sample below:

Original Simile List	**Mix and Match Simile List**
As restless as a salesman	As restless as pantyhose
As orange as Tang	As orange as taxes
As regular as taxes	As regular as a salesman
As hungry as a gorilla	As hungry as Tang
As pale as pantyhose	As pale as a gorilla
Smiling like a schoolgirl	Smiling like a lunatic
Grinning like a lunatic	Grinning like a schoolgirl

3. Begin a story, poem, or essay with one or more of the unusual similes you have created.

Excavating Instructions

1. Try mixing the adjectives and nouns you worked with above to create new metaphors, as in the sample list below. (A metaphor is a comparison made by asserting that one thing is another thing.)

Original List	**Mix and Match Metaphor List**
As rough as sandpaper	A first kiss is sandpaper.
As confining as an elevator	My prayer group is an elevator.
As tentative as a first kiss	The drunk is a new car.
As reliable as a new car	
Stumbling like a drunk	
Gathered together like a prayer group	

2. Begin an essay, poem, or story in which you work with one of the metaphors you have created, extending its definition and relevancy throughout the piece.

NUGGETS

A start on the poem "Family"
My sister is as fragile as a pill box
She makes herself tiny and empty
as yesterday's blue pliant moon

My brother is as restless
as an orange sock spinning
free from the dryer

I am praying like the taxman

DAVE THURMAN

From the essay "Dorm Room"
My dorm room is a bouquet. The florist has thrown it all in—the wild blues of laundry, the splashy orange of notebooks, the dry green of telephone lines. The fragrance lures them in from the hallway—the rich, delicate rendering of my roommate's boyfriend's cheap cologne, the slice of pepperoni pizza she saved from lunch, my Jergens skin cream.

RACHEL KAPLAN

ARTIFACTS

Harlem
What happens to a dream deferred?

Does it dry up
like a raisin in the sun?
Or fester like a sore—
And then run?
Does it stink like rotten meat?
Or crust and sugar over—
like a syrupy sweet?

Maybe it just sags like a heavy load.
Or does it explode?

LANGSTON HUGHES

implausible Causes and Unlikely Effects

In the natural course of things, any accident, event, development, phenomenon, or trend was caused by something else, just as any change from the status quo will produce one or several effects. Analysis of causes and effects is more often associated with science, engineering, and the insurance industry than with creative writing, but such analysis with a dash of imagination can produce some very engaging writing, including science fiction and mystery novels.

Anyone who has wondered how that single shoe found its way to the edge of the highway or how that car lost its sideview mirror has already begun the same process that mystery writers use to figure out how the murderer got in and out of the well-guarded hospital room. Anyone who has asked "What would it be like to be invisible for a day?" has already begun the process by which science fiction writers explore their many "what ifs." Poets and essayists also use such questions to begin poems and advance ideas. When William Stafford was asked how he came up with an idea for a poem wherein a bird spirals out of control, he said that one day he saw a bird and wondered how it would fly if it had only one wing. Of course it would fall, he realized, but for a while it would surely spiral.

The following exercises ask you to imaginatively indulge your natural curiosity and your prophetic powers to account for several extraordinary causes and effects.

Panning Instructions

Choose one or several of the following idea starters and imaginatively account for the causes of the phenomena described and/or provide a creative sequence of effects:

1. Two P.M. His wife never slept this late. (Why now?)
2. Someone had set his stuffed owl on fire. (Who and why?)
3. It would have been a perfect morning had she not noticed the neighbor's lawn chair sitting on her bed of ornamental cabbage. (How'd it get there? What happened?)

4. The note simply said "There are more where these came from." The only other things in the envelope were three perfectly clipped fingernails. (Whose fingernails? What's the meaning?)
5. This time she was grateful her husband hadn't noticed that she was wearing a new dress. (Why?)
6. The boys seemed to be kicking a large Bible between the two of them. (Why?)
7. The letter from the IRS said his returns for the previous three years would be examined. (What was his reaction?)
8. In the middle of the meeting, for no reason she could discern, she told her boss, "You have a lovely smile." (What happened?)
9. The ad he put in the paper included his phone number and simply said, "Send in the clowns." (What happened?)
10. It was tough fitting all those helium balloons in the station wagon. (What happened?)

☀️ Excavating Instructions

Sometimes extraordinary effects result from very ordinary occurrences, and very common results have very uncommon antecedents. Mispronouncing someone's name, or calling someone by the wrong name, can set off a lethal sequence of events. The simple salad your host presents to you might be the culmination of hellish dramas (for example, the first grocery store she went to might have been out of lettuce, the second store carried only lettuce that was so thoroughly wilted it couldn't be revived, and not one store in the whole town had decent cucumbers).

In this exercise, choose as a subject an ordinary cause, such as a change of address, or an ordinary effect, such as at last mastering the ability to whistle, and begin a story, poem, or essay that exposes or describes unlikely or dramatic antecedents or consequences. In Michael Jenkins's "One Way of Looking at It," notice how the ongoing effects of a dog bite changed the fortunes of a mail carrier (see below).

☆ NUGGETS

From the short story in progress "One Way of Looking at It"

I asked him what I thought to be a fairly typical question, one people must always ask of postmen: "Ever been bitten by a dog?"

He took a bite out of his grilled cheese sandwich and thought about my question as he chewed. "Oh, not too much trouble with dogs," he said. "Just once."

I had expected a couple of impassioned dog stories and was pleasantly surprised that Oscar had none.

But then he said, "Yep, a dog I'd known for maybe eight years. Surprised the bejesus out of me. Nice people, the owners."

"What happened?"

"Damnedest thing. I just put the mail in their box, same as I had done for years. Sometimes I'd see the dog, not a very big fella, a terrier of some sort, sometimes he wouldn't even come to the door. I'd petted that dog on hundreds of occasions. He knew me. Knew what I smelled like. But that day I put the mail in the box, as I said, and I hear the screen door close and next thing you know this little old dog bit me on the rear end."

Oscar laughed at this and shook his head.

He was silent after that, so I assumed he'd finished talking about it. I was preparing to change the subject and ask him about postal rates when he continued: "I really hated like the dickens to sue those folks. Nice people, as I said."

"You sued them?" It was hard to imagine this kindly man suing anybody, and from his description there didn't seem like much to sue over.

"Well, it wasn't so much me. The union, you know. Plus my co-workers, my boss. They thought I should. After I got out of the hospital . . ."

"Hospital?" I asked. "Why were you in the hospital?"

"Oh, one thing and another. Skin graft. Some muscle damage."

"From what?" I asked, thinking he was talking about something else now.

"Why the dog bite of course. That little fella hung on. Took a big bite out of my rear end. I was on my stomach for seven weeks. . . ."

"So you used the money from the lawsuit to buy the property in Santa Monica."

"That's right. And then I sold it and bought two more properties with the proceeds. My son manages one building. We made enough money to buy a place up in Malibu."

"Malibu? You bought a house in Malibu and three buildings in Santa Monica, all because of this dog bite?"

Oscar took a sip from his soda and looked at me with what seemed like genuine surprise.

"You know, I never thought of it that way. But you're right. That's certainly one way of looking at it."

MICHAEL JENKINS

 ARTIFACTS

From the short story "Any Minute Mom Should Come Blasting Through the Door"

Mom died in the middle of making me a sandwich. If I had known it was going to kill her, I never would have asked. It never killed her before to make a sandwich, so why all of a sudden. My dad didn't understand it either. But we don't talk about it too much. Sometimes we try. Sometimes it's just the two of us at dinner, and things are almost good.

But only sometimes.

DAVID ORDAN

Assaying:
How Do You Know It's Gold?

There was one person in the camp, and only one, who had seen gold in pieces new from the earth. This was Jenny Wimmer. Not only had Jenny seen virgin gold, but she knew how women tested it in their backwoods kitchens. . . . Jenny took Jim's bits of metal and soaked them in vinegar. They came out unhurt. Now, she told the men, she would try a test more severe. Jenny was boiling a kettle of soap, strong lye soap that would take the dirt and sweat out of men's work clothes. She dropped some bits of metal into her lye vat and let it boil all day and simmer all night. Nothing but gold, said Jenny, could stand the test.

From Golden Dreams, *by Gwen Bristow*

If you have attempted several of the exercises in this book, you have generated many ideas and beginnings for stories, poems, and essays. *Beginnings, in the way we are using the term here, are not necessarily the same as the starts of poems, stories, or essays. Your beginnings may in fact end up in the middle or end of your final poem, story, or essay, or they might be replaced altogether with new writing.* Perhaps you have even gone beyond beginnings to fully develop several pieces. But if you haven't, a question you're likely to have at this point is, "What do I do with all this writing?"

What you do with the material you have generated is, of course, up to you. You may have had fun doing the exercises for their own sake, and that's enough for now. On the other hand, you may want to continue to work on a piece and shape it into a specific form—a story, poem, or essay. Review "From Nuggets to Artifacts What Form Should You Choose?" on page 20. But first you need to decide which pieces to work on further. How can you tell which exercises resulted in the most promising material?

Unlike the methods for assaying metals for gold, there is no guaranteed way of determining beforehand whether a piece of writing contains gold. In the realm of art and creativity, it's nearly impossible to get any two people to agree on criteria for evaluating whether something is good. Even if they reach an agreement, the next hurdle is getting these same people to agree that something does or doesn't meet the criteria. Add to these difficulties the fact that the exercises being looked at here are simply beginnings, and it's clear that any "objective" criteria that might be applied to a finished piece of writing should be considered only very cautiously.

Still, you need some way to begin to sift through the sand and rock and jackrabbit bones you have dug up. The following recommendations, then, are given in the spirit of helping you to separate the gold from the dross.

- **Respect how you feel about a beginning.** If you are in love with something you wrote and you have a tremendous hunch that it could pan out, you almost have no choice but to pursue it. Your task and problem here are similar to Michelangelo's when he tried to find the slabs of Carrara marble that would contain his visions for his sculptures. Sometimes he would have a two-ton piece of marble carted back to his studio and work on the piece for days, only to discover that his figures would not emerge from the marble the way he had imagined them. He had no choice but to destroy these and return to the quarry. Fortunately, more often than not, Michelangelo's instincts were correct, and undoubtedly he got better at choosing with time and experience. Since your medium is words, the stakes are not quite as high in choosing the rough beginnings that will flourish into finished stories, poems, or essays.

- **Show your work to someone you respect.** Obviously, if you are taking a writing class, the writing instructor would probably fill this role, as might classmates whose opinions you trust. Most experienced writers and writing teachers will be able to look over your exercises and pick out a few that seem promising, in addition to offering some tips for how to develop the pieces. Otherwise, consider showing your work to someone whose opinion you value and who, ideally, reads extensively or is very interested in writing. People who are not devoted friends will probably be reluctant to comment on your work in general but may feel better about looking over a few beginnings and choosing the ones that they'd like to see developed. Be careful about showing personal pieces to the people whom they are about, especially too early in the process. Their opinions about the work may be distorted by any personal biases they have.

DOES IT GLITTER: FRESHNESS AND ORIGINALITY

Aside from your own or someone else's sense about your beginnings, the following factors might suggest that you continue.

The Topic or Piece of Writing Keeps Coming Back to You

If something you have written virtually haunts you, this may be a strong indication that you should develop it. Once, in the course of freewriting, one of the coauthors wrote the phrase "It was no ordinary parasol, officer." The sound and rhythm of that odd phrase returned to him almost every time he sat down to write. It would even come to him as he sat watching a movie. The problem was that it made no sense to him. It was just an intriguing fragment. But he had this powerful sense that it could become something. He worked on it off and on for nearly two years and finally finished and ultimately published a poem about a prostitute in the French Quarter of New Orleans. He did not work nonstop on this piece for two years. He worked on other pieces as well, and so should you, even if one beginning particularly haunts you.

You Find Yourself "Working" on the Piece Without Deliberately Trying To

Perhaps you began the "At the Checkout Line" exercise and were delighted with some of the items you placed upon the imaginary conveyor belt—to such a degree that while at work on your job you imagined yet other odd and fascinating items on it . . . a buffalo's beard, a pirate's eyepatch, an inflatable Pat Sajak. Or perhaps you began describing your best friend's talent at mixing up people's names while doing "The Evolution of Mini-Skills" exercise, and now you are on the phone talking to someone else about this realization, supplying examples, elaborating. In both instances, it might be better to stop what you're doing, if you can, and develop the piece. In such cases, your writing imagination is still crackling synapses, and it's always a shame to waste that kind of energy.

The Beginning of the Piece Helped You Discover Something You Didn't Know About Yourself or Someone Else or the Human Condition

Many of the preceding writing exercises ask you to reflect about yourself, your sense of the world, and your experiences in it. In completing the "Mixing Relationships" exercise, perhaps you discovered that there are a number of things that you don't do with your spouse that you do with others—perhaps for no good reason. The exercise allowed you to touch on this, but developing the piece might show you the way to work through it, at least on paper. Such realizations in writing make for very powerful stories, poems, and essays. (Writing can be and is therapeutic for many, though we don't recommend restricting it to that role.)

You Are Intrigued by an Odd or Original Connection You Have Made Between Two Seemingly Very Different Things

The essence of metaphor is transformation, relating one aspect of experience to another and thereby altering both; for example, Emily Dickinson imagined the hummingbird as a mail carrier from Tunisia; Ezra Pound imagined the faces of people at a subway station as "white petals on a wet black bough." In both cases, two very different realities are related, and the result enriches our perception and sense of both. Many of the preceding exercises involve you in metaphors of one kind or another, and it is very likely that you came up with metaphors that for the first time connected two very different phenomena in a rewarding fashion.

You Introduced a Character You Like a Great Deal and Are Concerned About What Might Happen to Her or Him

In the course of completing exercises involving descriptions of people, real and fictional, you may on occasion find yourself invested in a character's fate. You wonder how the character you have created will handle a certain problem. As you struggle through your own daily dilemmas, you find yourself anticipating the way one of your characters might react. Fiction writers often care nearly as much about the characters they've created as they do about their real friends and family. (In the course of writing the novel *Beloved*, Toni Morrison has said she felt that her characters literally had moved in with her.) This is only natural since in a very real sense the writer gives birth to characters and cares as only a parent can care.

If you have such feelings about a character or characters you have brought to life on paper, this is a good sign that you should stick with the piece.

You Introduced a Character You Dislike and Are Concerned About the Damage He or She May Do

Sometimes we create people whom we hope *never* to meet in real life. While total villains are often one-dimensional and can easily fall into the category of clichéd or stock characters, brooding, neurotic, mean-spirited, narcissistic, vindictive people often set stories into motion and, if fully developed, can make wonderful characters.

As a writer, it's your job to see the humanity in even the most loathsome of creations. While you may not love these creatures, to avoid creating clichéd characters it's important that you understand them and their motivations and realize that we all have something in common. Even a mass murderer probably has a favorite breakfast cereal, not to mention a mother, father, or sibling who worries about him.

If you have created a character whom you don't particularly like but who nevertheless intrigues you, you may very well have the beginnings of a compelling piece of writing.

You Love the Sound of the Words
You Have Strung Together

Beginning writing efforts are often marked by flourishes of remarkable words, phrases, and rhythms. Sometimes the meanings are not all that satisfying, but the sounds may be beautiful and compelling, and this may signal that you should continue with the piece.

You Feel Like You Could Write a Lot More About This

While your final essays, stories, and poems will vary in length greatly—many writers feel that each piece they write has its own natural length—if you feel you could write a lot initially on the subject, that is certainly a good sign. This means that the topic has sparked something that resonates with either your imagination, your life experience, or a combination of the two.

You may end up using a small fraction of all of this outpouring of words, but for most writers it is generally easier to edit by cutting back than by adding on to a meager start.

You're Dying to Send/Show the Piece to Others

Wanting to share work is a clear sign that a writer is excited about her material. At heart, most adults are not so different from children who eagerly choose what amazing new thing to bring in for show-and-tell to share with their classmates. If you want others to see or hear your work, usually this means there is something in it worth working on further.

Of course, there are exceptions. Perhaps you want to show someone your initial work on "Mixing Relationships" strictly because you think he'll get a kick out of the fact that he appears in it. Still, even in these kinds of cases, that genuine spark of interest may be there.

You Feel That What You Have
Written Is Fresh or Original

With respect to writing, most people agree that freshness, originality, and an element of surprise are factors in what they characterize as "creative." Ben Jonson, a seventeenth-century English writer and scholar, characterized poetry as "What has been oft thought but ne'r so well expressed." In so saying, Jonson relieves poets of the obligation of coming up with new ideas and focuses on the perhaps infinite number of ways that ideas can be expressed.

To illustrate this idea, consider that most of us were required to write a "What I Did This Summer" essay at some point in our school careers. While the subject matter for these essays is largely the same among classmates—camp, swimming pools, summer jobs—the ways in which we wrote our stories, those details we chose to highlight and those we chose to omit, are what gave each piece its own flavor and perhaps its shot at originality. Compare, for example, the first paragraph of the following hypothetical "What I Did This Summer" essays written by two sixth-graders who had largely the same summer experiences:

1. I went to camp this summer, which was interesting. I had never been to camp before and I enjoyed meeting new people. I slept in a bunk house with five other girls. I went sailing and learned how to macramé, which really is more boring than it might sound. I made a new friend who was very nice. We did a lot of activities together, which made everything a little more interesting than it was before. It's important to have a good friend at camp.

2. Has anyone ever tried to convince you that tying knots is fun? How about sitting on a stagnant pond waiting for a gust of wind that never comes? Well, I spent the summer waiting to be convinced that either of these activities were fun. At least I made a friend, Bobbie. Finally, we got smart and started hiding behind the bunk and reading her sister's old issues of *Seventeen* when it was time for knot-tying class—whoops, I mean macramé.

Most people would say that the second sixth-grader's beginning is much more compelling than the first's. The difference lies in the freshness of detail. Notice how the first writer relies heavily on words such as *boring, interesting,* and even *nice* that are overused and not as specific as they could be. She seems to be merely fulfilling the assignment instead of having fun with it.

The second writer, on the other hand, seems more engaged with her material. While she apparently found macramé at least as fulfilling as the first writer did, she doesn't bore the reader with her description of it. Instead she pokes fun, calling it "knot tying," and finally lets us in on the joke. While the first writer tells us that her friendship was important to her, the second writer shows us what the friendship was like and how it helped redeem camp for her. Finally, notice that the second writer leaves out details that are not particularly telling, such as that she slept in a bunk house and met a lot of new people. As she focused on the liveliest part of her camp experience, the more typical details naturally vanished.

In your own writing, look for pieces that have the kind of freshness illustrated by the second example, or that seem capable of it. Remember, the situation itself need not be unusual, as long as your rendering of it causes the reader to look at it in a new way.

You Believe That What You Have Written Honestly Expresses Some of Your Feelings

Whether you're working on fiction, poetry, or creative nonfiction, honesty of expression is equally important. By honesty, we don't mean that you write only about what really happened. Actual events and experiences don't always translate into the best poem or story. Even essays usually benefit from selective editing of the facts.

Writing that is emotionally honest doesn't gloss over feelings, even those that may disturb the writer. Writing that is emotionally honest isn't always neat or pretty, but it is always emotionally true.

In looking over her work on "The Backpack," one writer, who was adopted as an infant, came across the following passage that she had written about a photograph of herself and her birth mother—a photograph that she had carried in her purse since their "reunion" a year before:

> *Our faces squeeze close as we grin into the camera, faking delight at the similarity of our features. That crooked grin I always wondered about. Our reunion. We pretend this is it—family. I never thought I'd meet you, first, fleeting mother. We are an odd match, more like two strangers who resemble each other than relatives. You are not the one I call mother. I don't know if I want to see you again. I don't know why I save this photograph.*

Although this passage made her uncomfortable, she felt that it expressed her conflicted feelings in an emotionally honest way and that the piece might be rich material for developing into an essay or poem.

Honesty of expression also does not include sentimentality, which is the emotional equivalent of a cliché (see the section on "Clichéd Emotions: Sentimentality" on page 184) and is used more often to manipulate and hide emotions than to express them.

You Have Created Tension or Conflict

You may think that the only kind of writing that requires conflict is fiction. But that's not really the case. Most writing that engages the reader contains tension or conflict of *some kind;* otherwise, it can seem boring and facile. "That's nice," followed by a big yawn is not the reaction you want your readers to have.

The tension you create in your work may be purely internal; the narrator or a character explores a psychological or emotional concern. Or it may be external—the narrator or a character is in conflict with another person or her environment. Often it is a combination of the two, as Robert Mettler discovered as he reread the draft of his poem "Don't Ask Me," which was based on the "Quilting" exercise.

Don't Ask Me

Don't ask me about the red.
The hem of the bright red orlon sweater
given me one Christmas
became hopelessly caught in a carnivorous
zipper and appalled my lovely third grade teacher.

Don't ask me about the white.
The collar of my best white shirt
should have had lipstick on it
but remained as virginal as a priest
who was really a saint.

ROBERT METTLER

In the first stanza, Robert describes the literal tension of the sweater caught in the pants zipper coupled with his teacher's reaction, as well as his feelings for his "lovely" teacher—a whole brew of conflicts there. In the second stanza, the tensions arise in a different way. They are more abstract this time, but still integral to the piece: the lack of the lipstick, the stain that wasn't there but should have been there. Tension existed in that discrepancy.

Consider working on pieces that are already on their way to creating one or another kind of tension or conflict. Such writing is ready for development.

HOW TO SORT REAL GOLD FROM FOOL'S GOLD

Be Sure That What You Have Written Doesn't Descend into Cliché

Clichéd Subjects. While the subject you choose to write about doesn't have to be unusual, you should be aware that stock situations often give rise to clichés, as much as you may try to avoid them. A clichéd subject is one that is so typical that it has become trite or one that is little more than a stereotype. For example, a story about a rich heiress named Tiffany who lives in Beverly Hills and has a Hispanic servant who is sleeping with the gardener is probably too clichéd for most writers to redeem. Similarly, an essay about the faithful collie you had as a boy, who constantly rescued you from danger, or a poem about the beauty of a rose stand little chance of exploring fresh territory.

Clichéd Characters. Just as subjects can be clichéd, so can characterizations. A fat man who breathes heavily or sweats copiously; a chain-smoking (or sucker-sucking) private detective; a bored, minivan-driving housewife; and a recent immigrant who minces the language are all examples of stock or clichéd characters. It's not that such people do not exist; of course they do. It's just that they have been described so often and so superficially that they appear more as stereotypes than as real people. If you have begun to develop characters in your exercises, ferret out those who might be based on clichés by trying to imagine going out to lunch with each of them. Do they sit there like stick figures, only saying stock phrases? Do you find it hard to get them talking at all? It's the multidimensional or rounded characters with whom you will be able to carry on the conversation, while the clichéd characters silently chain-smoke or sweat, with no thoughts or feelings of their own to share.

Clichéd Emotions: Sentimentality. While it has been said that writing of any worth approaches sentimentality, good writing steers just clear of plummeting into it in a blubbering mass.

Sentimentality is clichéd emotion. Nearly everybody wept when Ali McGraw died in *Love Story* and when Debra Winger slowly wasted away in *Terms of Endearment*. In the first case, a beautiful young woman was "shot down in her prime"; in the second case, we watched a young, vibrant mother of two adorable children die an agonizingly slow death. How could we not cry? Still, hours later, along with the enduring flavor of greasy popcorn, the taste of something else may have lingered, the residue of manipulation.

Good readers want to be genuinely moved, not manipulated. The difference is sometimes subtle. If your intention in writing a particular piece is strictly to move someone no matter which way your material seems to be naturally headed, you may be indulging in sentimentality.

Clichéd Language. Perhaps the kind of cliché you are most familiar with is clichéd language. (If you worked on the exercise "The Cliché's the Thing," you experimented with identifying and exploiting clichéd language.) It is a cliché to write that someone "laughed until he cried" or had "ants in her pants." Sometimes we come up with what seem like wonderful expressions only to find out they are clichés.

The problem with clichés is that while they're often poetic-sounding, they're rarely completely accurate. Someone who writes that she had "stars in her eyes" the night she met her boyfriend may really have had beer in her stomach and a furious urge to dance with the next person who asked her. Someone who writes that he had "butterflies" when at the age of fifty-five he gave his first clarinet recital may have really been crunching so methodically on hard candy before he got on stage that all he could think about was brushing his teeth.

Look through your own beginnings for situations, characters, and passages in which you might have easily succumbed to cliché but didn't. The fact that you didn't shows you have a level of care and concern for this material that could help lead you to a strong finished piece.

Beware of What Too Easily Amuses or Impresses You

While many writers are their own toughest critics, these same writers can, on occasion, be too easily wowed by their own work. You may write a line that bowls you over with its humor or sentiment each time you read it, only to find that it is nearly impossible to develop the piece in such a way that lets anyone else in on what is essentially a private joke or revelation.

Reading over the work he did on the exercise "Around the Water Cooler," one writer was delighted to discover he had created the following rumor about his office mate:

> When working on the Davis account, Jeannine heard the word of God guiding her through the paperwork.

Each time he read this passage over, he actually laughed aloud, thinking about the organized Jeannine with her briefcase and datebook being guided spiritually at work. Assuming that no one else could resist this image, the writer read the line to his wife, only to find her staring blankly back at him. He tried again, reading the line to another office mate; this time he received a polite half-smile and a mumbled question about whether he was ordering in for lunch. Why didn't anyone else get it?

The problem here is not that the image of a very practical person suddenly becoming spiritual couldn't be developed into a compelling description for a story, poem, or essay; it just hasn't yet. The connections the writer has made in his mind haven't been made on the page because he is so taken with his insight that he hasn't seen that it is still strictly personal, his insight alone.

When you come across a private "joke" of some kind in your work, decide whether the piece of writing is really meant to be private, an "in-joke" just you and perhaps one close friend appreciate, or whether you're ready to step back and make the necessary connections to reveal its significance and meaning to the rest of the world.

SOME FINAL THOUGHTS

Now that you have been warned about what to avoid, remember that all writers, even the most well-published and experienced, at times descend into cliché or find themselves perhaps too easily impressed by their initial drafts. While it's part of every writer's job to learn to separate the gold from the dross, its unrealistic to expect every effort you make to pan out.

In fact, most practicing writers have drawers or file cabinets full of sand, rocks, and jackrabbit bones: short stories that never quite came to life; poems waiting for their finishing stanzas; essay ideas that didn't gel; even entire novels that for whatever reason didn't "work." Still, these efforts are much more than simple wastes of time. Even the stories, poems, and essays we will never finish can lead us mysteriously to our next stories, poems, or essays.

The important thing to remember is that as long as you are writing and engaging what is truly unique in you, you will always be approaching the best in all writing. Contrary to what many people think, the writing that is most affecting does not necessarily consist of the wildest and most extravagant imaginings by those who lead wild and extravagant lives, but instead consists of unique and very personal takes on everyday experiences.

From Nuggets to Artifacts: Finishing What You Started

For many writers, the "fun" part of writing ends with the first draft or paragraph or stanza. When the initial inspiration ends, all too often words fail to flow as easily, characters begin to bore, scenes close up too quickly. The writer sees a blank page or computer screen and wills the phone to ring, discovers how desperately the vegetable bin needs to be cleaned, conducts an Internet search on Beanie Babies to see if her son's collection might finance his college education even with the swing tags missing. Finally, the writer decides a walk might do both her and her dog good, and while yelling at her dog to drop the chicken bone he's found under a picnic table in the park, she suddenly hears her character yelling at her cat for sleeping on the new bedspread right before her husband walks in with the news that he's been fired. She reins in her dog and hurries home and sits down at her computer, no more confident about where the story she's working on will end up, but now ready to at least open the next scene.

When we're actively writing, we're writing even when we're not writing, but don't fool yourself: you still have to sit down at the computer or typewriter to melt down, hammer, and shape the nuggets you have joyfully gathered.

While the intent of this book is to outfit you with what you need to discover the nuggets, veins, and mother lodes of images, ideas, plots, and theories within you, you will probably find at some point that while you have started many inspired pieces, you have yet to finish any of them. Genius, as Thomas Edison said, "is 1 percent inspiration and 99 percent perspiration," and now you are facing the real effort—though not necessarily a disagreeable or painful effort—involved with writing anything worthwhile. This stage of the writing process contains many steps and tasks, including organizing, developing, revising, editing, proofreading and, possibly, publishing.

It is likely that on occasion you will get stuck or perhaps discouraged with your progress. Some writers have compared these points to the *wall* that long-distance runners experience, a point at which your entire being is commanding or imploring you just to quit. The bad news about the *wall* is that it is very persuasive and has taken its toll. The good news is that, as experienced runners and writers know, beyond that point lie the real rewards of the endeavor, and if you keep pushing, it is likely that extraordinary things will happen. To return to the overarching metaphor in this book, the extraordinary may rise stunningly out of what you at first considered to be ordinary, mundane, or prosaic, so whatever you do, don't give up.

The following tips are intended to help you get unstuck when you are stuck and run through the *walls* or writer's blocks that rise before you.

When You Get Stuck Writing a Poem

Play Out the Language

It may seem almost too obvious a thing to say, but poetry is about words. It is not, primarily, about communication, meaning, or ideas. While poets hope their readers find meaning and beauty in what they write, their primal contract is between themselves and language. The best poets forge new relationships between experience and language. Therefore, when you get stuck, a valid and genuine thing to do is to build upon each word, phrase, or expression you have already written, to go back, as it were, and play out these words and images. To play them out, isolate the words and expressions you have come up with and take off on or repeat the sounds in the words, look them up in a dictionary and let the definitions send you off to new places, or allow personal associations to supply words. For example, you have arrived, after already great effort, at the following five lines, but have no idea where to go from here:

> The hagfish
> has five hearts
> all strung within its primitive
> dark frame
> like a constellation of cherries . . .

You wrote this stanza because you were intrigued with this creature and the fact that it has five hearts, a characteristic of deep-sea creatures, whose anatomy must withstand great pressure. You have tried to develop the relationship between having so many hearts and living at great depth under enormous pressure, but so far nothing satisfactory has come of it—which isn't to say that nothing will come of it. It just hasn't so far.

The language, however, has taken you into the night skies, and since you are there, perhaps there are hagfish or perhaps the stars are the hearts of those who lived under great pressure, the greatest pressure perhaps occurring in black holes, where, you discover through research, the gravity is so great not even light can escape. Perhaps the hagfish should be added to the zodiac, for certainly people have been born under a sign of invisible stars. Whole lives have been lived in the primitive dark frame. And here is the opportunity for a leap from what started as the subject into a completely new realm. You write

    the astrological sign
    of people who never get started
    like Otis Hatfield

    the meanest kid in the first and second grade
    the smallest in the third and then on
    and the meekest and sweetest after the steel plate.

    As astonished as I was to lose my early fear
    of him, how astonished those who loved him
    must have been

    a janitor now in the same school
    for years
    born under the sign of the hagfish
    with seven good years under his belt
    whistling the one song he learned
    all heart now
    just heart.

As this poem has developed, the astrological aspect of the opening has been played out; a personal association, Otis Hatfield, rises out of it.

It may seem as though this is a process that could go on ad infinitum, and "When is enough enough?" becomes the question. While there are no universal, objective criteria for determining when a poem is finished, it is likely that if you continue in this fashion a kind of gestalt will occur, a point at which all the parts—the words, their sounds, the images, the form, the meaning—all gather into a whole that is greater than the sum of the parts. As a writer, you may recognize this point when your engagement with the substance of the poem naturally abates, which is not the same as giving up or quitting. There quite simply is no more to say. It is as though the poem in process is now a finished sphere. Any attempt to add or take away anything will seem a trespass. Beginning writers should beware, however. This is an *earned* feeling, and is far different from simply falling in love with any words you have arranged on the page in the shape of a poem.

To commit yourself to writing poetry is to act on a faith that such spheres exist in or may emerge from your ideas and inspirations. Ultimately, when you get stuck, it is this faith that will keep you keeping on, to paraphrase Bob Dylan.

Choose Random Words from Another Source

Open up the first novel you see. Go to page 23 and find the first and last complete sentences on the page. Attach both sentences to the end of the point where you got stuck and edit and change them around to make them fit somehow.

If you chose *Beloved* by Toni Morrison, in the paperback edition, the first complete sentence is "They stood back and waited for her to put it on the ground (at the foot of a tree) and leave." The last sentence on page 23 is "Seth had the amazing luck of six whole years of marriage to that 'somebody' son who had fathered every one of her children."

The hagfish
has five hearts
all strung within its primitive
dark frame
like a constellation of cherries . . .
The Portuguese fishermen stood back
and waited for her to explode
as they sometimes do.

The hagfish has the amazing luck
of six whole years of marriage to that
"somebody" son who had fathered every one
of her children.

The result may lead you to explore other subjects, themes, modes, or points of view. In the above example, the random sentences bring up the issue of children, marriage, and the possibility of another point of view. In this case the pronoun "they" was given the antecedent of "Portuguese fishermen."

Any book could serve this purpose, any page number or paragraph. You could use the Bible or an art dictionary. The idea is to get unstuck, and using random words and selections can release you from the grip of too much consciousness.

Of course, if you do lift phrases and sentences, be sure to work with the material and make it yours. To leave these words and expressions in their original form may require acknowledgment and permission if you decide to publish the results.

Start Saying the Opposite

Refuting or turning around the last thing you said can result in a whole new direction:

A hagfish without a heart
collapses on itself
the victim of its element . . .

Repeat the Last Word, Phrase, Line, or Stanza
Sometimes simply by repeating the last words, lines, phrases, or stanzas, new relationships or images can emerge, as in the following:

The hagfish
has five hearts
all strung within its primitive
dark frame
like a constellation of cherries,
cherries overripe and black now
a constellation of black holes . . .

Repeating the words "cherries" and "constellation" prompts the writer to say something else about them, in this case leading to the idea of black holes.

Rhyme the Last Line and Move in the Direction of the Rhymed Word
There's nothing like a rhyme scheme to draw a poem into other orbits, and introducing rhyme in the middle of a poem is a good way of doing so without necessarily being constrained by a verse form.

The hagfish has five hearts all strung
in its dark frame like Saratoga cherries.
When it rises to the surface, it carries
the compounded pressure of its lungs.

Transpose the First Stanza and the Last Stanza
Quite often writers discover in their early drafts that the place at which a poem supposedly ends is the most interesting part. In essence, everything up to that end is a kind of flexing or prewriting. Also, some writers' imaginations work in reverse chronology. Simply because your consciousness dictated the order of a poem, don't assume that your imagination works this way. Always consider starting with the last stanza and ending with the first stanza of your draft.

Inject a Memory or a Dream
Memories and dreams often find themselves in a poem anyway, but if you get stuck, consider deliberately calling up a distant or recent memory or dream and including it.

WHEN YOU GET STUCK WRITING A STORY

Add a Character

So your two main characters, ex-lovers who are now trying to remain friends, are sitting down in a restaurant discussing their plans for the holidays. Both are careful not to mention any new names. In fact, they're being exceedingly polite to each other, so polite that they're beginning to bore you to distraction. Add a distraction. Have one of their new romances walk into the restaurant and, uninvited, join them. Have a cell phone ring in a coat breast pocket and a teenage son you didn't know either of them had announce that he needs a money order sent for three hundred dollars to a certain address immediately.

Let Your Characters Lead

A question frequently asked in fiction workshops is: Whose story is this? While the answer to this question will vary from story to story, one answer experienced writers can be immediately certain of is, once on the page, their stories are no longer theirs.

Our stories belong to our characters. We may invent these folks, but, as writers, we need to give them permission to take over, to lead us off in directions we may not have chosen or imagined. Otherwise, our characters do not come to life; instead, they remain mere devices we employ to transmit plots we had already fully imagined. And we end up with dry stories and flat characters.

When you're feeling stuck, ask your characters where to go. Take them with you as you go about the rest of your day. Notice how they respond to situations you find yourself in. Sit back down at your desk and allow them to continue on their way.

Create a Scene

Your story may feel stuck because you're summarizing instead of allowing your writing to open up into full-blown scenes. Make your characters move. Have them pace the room, yell at each other, create a scene.

Keep to the moment. Whether you're writing in past tense or present tense, the bulk of your story should be happening in the "now." Delete all phrases such as "I remember," "As I recall," "Usually," "Sometimes," "Often." Delete all flashbacks that are not absolutely necessary, and, if a flashback is absolutely necessary, write it with the same urgency and detail you bring to the present moment.

Add Weather

Most of us are familiar with how weather can become its own cliché—"It was a dark and stormy night"—but if your story is feeling dead to you, you might want to consider resuscitating it by making sure the characters are living in a real environment, instead of a glass bubble. Rain doesn't have to make your characters feel depressed, but it may cause one of them to slop mud all over a freshly mopped entrance hall in a brand new house in a spanking new development where only one of them had wanted to live in the first place, and, then, who knows what might happen next.

Add Trouble

While you may wish your friends and yourself only the best, you need to wish your characters trouble. Not necessarily grand-scale, cataclysmic trouble—which is often hard to write about in a way that feels authentic—but trouble of the more mundane variety. Philandering spouses, relentless bill collectors, clueless real estate agents, truant schoolchildren all should haunt your characters' lives on a regular basis. Mess up the surface of their happiness. Lay them bare.

Raise the Stakes

"Who cares?" may be one of life's great existential questions, but this is not a question you want readers asking after reading one of your stories. If you're feeling stuck, perhaps it's because *you* don't care. Get invested. Ask yourself in the most humble way possible why this moment you have somehow chosen to write about matters. For example, who cares (do you?) when your character, an insomniac college student, finally works up the nerve to ask out the waitress at the all-night Denny's? But what if this same character has lusted after this particular waitress for close to a year before finally finding the courage to ask her out on a date? And what if this same character hasn't had a date since he was unceremoniously dumped back in high school?

Add a Second Story

If you're feeling stuck with your first story line, add a second one. Most stories we admire have at least two running plots happening simultaneously. Consider, for example, the short story "A Small Good Thing" by Raymond Carver. In this story, the central plot concerns a young boy who is hit by a car, feels fine for several hours, and then falls into a coma from which he never recovers. The second plot revolves around a baker who becomes increasingly irritated and irrational as the story progresses because the boy's parents fail to pick up a cake he's prepared for the boy's birthday. Of course, the baker has no idea initially that the boy is dying in the hospital. The two story lines eventually connect. Don't worry about how yours will connect as you start a second one. Worry later.

WHEN YOU GET STUCK WRITING A CREATIVE ESSAY

Interview Someone
If you're writing about your childhood, interview your old neighbors, your piano teacher, your camp counselor. Hunt people down through phone books, court records, word-of-mouth. Be a good reporter, asking them questions that are impossible to answer with only a yes or a no. Let their recollections guide your interview questions. Be prepared to allow your creative essay to take a new direction if you feel yourself being led on a route that intrigues you.

Interview Yourself
You may surprise yourself with your answers. What *did* you think of moving into that new house where you finally had your own bedroom? Answer honestly. If you don't feel too self-conscious to do this, try taping your interview instead of writing your responses. Many of us who write are more likely to worry about how our answers "sound" in writing than in how they actually sound aloud.

Look Up Unusual Facts Surrounding Your Subject
If, for example, you're writing an essay about your parents' divorce in 1970, look up the top fall fashion tips from the August 1970 issue of *Vogue*, or another fashion magazine, and begin your essay with those. Be creative. Don't worry yet about how these "facts" will ultimately connect with what you're writing.

Employ Fictional Techniques
Try incorporating dialogue—obviously, you will be taking creative license here. Write in the "now," avoiding such phrases as "I remember."

Begin Your Next Paragraph with a Particular Moment
Start your next paragraph with the phrase "One day" and then make a particular moment happen. Don't allow hazy memories to make your writing hazy.

Create a Bold, New Organizing Strategy
To keep going on a creative essay that feels stuck, try organizing sections with the names of street signs or cigarette brands or song titles or motel names.

For example, if you're writing about the small Ohio town you grew up in and the way that town turned your mother first into a churchgoer—she loved singing in the choir, any choir—and then into a drunk—after she had worked her way through the churches, she began to work her way through the bars—you might consider organizing your essay with the names of the churches and the bars in that small town. Perhaps you would begin by interspersing the two, as in the following list:

Church of God
Jack's Bar and Grill
Highway House of Worship
Dolly's

These headings would serve as initial section headings of your essay.

Take a Trip

If you're writing about a place or time that is distant, travel there. Perhaps this means loading up your car and driving or buying a plane ticket to the town where you first met the subject of your essay. But, if time or finances or life circumstances don't allow this, your trip may be more of the metaphoric variety. Pull out dusty photo albums and peel tape away from stored boxes. Surround yourself not just with visual reminders from a time and place you hope to evoke in an essay, but try to surround yourself with scents and sounds from that period or place as well. Pull out old records and play them instead of listening to the news while you make dinner. Buy incense at the flea market and turn your bedroom into your old dorm room.

When You Get Stuck in General

Don't Insist on Knowing Where You're Going

Psychologists have noted that children who claim to be bored are often simply overwhelmed with the possibilities of what they might do next. As writers, it's important to keep this idea in mind as we tire of the pieces we have begun but not yet finished. Often, we feel stuck simply when we don't know what's going to happen next, and we're afraid of the endless possibilities.

Let your story, poem, or essay head off into several different directions at once. Don't insist on any one of these. You will have time to evaluate later which path seems the most promising. Let go of your control. Be surprised by where you are led.

Use Exercises in this Book as Prompts for Scenes, Stanzas, or New Ideas

Start a new exercise from this book in the middle of working on your story, poem, or essay. Open the book to any page and choose your exercise at random. If applicable, answer the prompts for this new exercise in character. Incorporate at least part of this new material into the next paragraph or stanza of your work in progress.

Start a List

Starting a list at a point at which you get stuck can initiate creative momentum and lead to new angles and ideas. Listing can speed ahead of consciousness and forge exotic paths.

Start in the Middle of the Story, Poem, or Essay

This is advice often given to writers of stories, but it applies equally well to poets. Eight times out of ten, you will be better off getting rid of your first stanza and beginning with the second or even the third. Doing this can sometimes supply new sources of energy.

Shift Something: Point of View, Time Period, Voice, or Tone

Shifting some aspect of your writing in process can open up exciting vistas. In the following example, the point of view is shifted from third to first person, unleashing a whole new set of possibilities for the developing poem.

> The hagfish
> has five hearts
> all strung within its primitive
> dark frame
> like a constellation of cherries.
>
> I have had them for breakfast,
> a great way to start the day
> or end a relationship.

While it can be invigorating to shift key elements while work is in process, keep in mind that *completed* short stories and essays generally rely on a consistent point of view, time period, and tone.

Write About What Is Going On in or Around You at the Moment You Get Stuck

In John Ashberry's poem "Self-Portrait in A Convex Mirror," the subject is the artist Francesco Parmigianino and the process the artist may have used to paint his self-portrait. Ashberry meditates on how the painter's pencil was affected or modulated by what was going on around him so that in the pencil strokes and angles time is preserved. The poet addresses his own writing process and relates it to Parmigianino's:

> I think of the friends
> Who came to see me, of what yesterday
> Was like. A peculiar slant
> Of memory that intrudes on the dreaming model
> In the silence of the studio as he considers
> Lifting the pencil to the self-portrait:
> How many people came and stayed a certain time,
> Uttered light or dark speech that became part of you [the self-portrait]

Don't discount the here and now as a source of ideas. Include the sound of trucks and barking dogs outside your window; they can give rise to a curve of thought, a stroke of genius.

Stop Writing in the Middle of a Scene, Stanza, or Line

Perhaps the best tip we can give is one that helps you avoid ever getting stuck in the first place. While it may feel counterintuitive, stop writing at exactly the place at which you want to keep going. That is, when you know just what the next scene, line, or word should be, stop typing or writing. Not only will you be eager to get back to work at the next opportunity you have, you will know exactly how to begin where you left off.

Gold Futures:
Prospects for Publication

While this book is concerned primarily with launching creative writing projects, we hope some of these beginnings will be shaped and developed into compelling finished stories, poems, and essays. Although we do not advocate becoming overly concerned about publication early in a writing project—or early in your own development as a writer—the point will come when you may want to share your work with a broader audience than your class, friends, or family. You will be happy to know that there are hundreds of publications out there seeking quality work. Indeed, for the best writing there is always a home in one publication or another. However, if you decide to submit your work for publication, you should brace yourself for rejection. In fact, rejection is so much a part of the publication process that most writers figure on sending their work out many times before finally seeing it published. The following are tips for how to find appropriate publishers and how to prepare and send your most polished manuscripts.

FINDING A HOME FOR YOUR WORK

Determining the best place to send your work depends both on the nature of your work and your ambitions. If you are writing poems, stories, and creative nonfiction essays, your best bet is to pursue publication in little magazines and journals with small but literate and discerning readerships. The few well-known national publications that accept such work, such as *The Atlantic, The New Yorker,* and *The Nation,* receive tens of thousands of submissions. Send to such well-known publications bearing in mind that the odds of the work of a new writer being accepted are infinitesimally slim. However, some of the highest quality writing in the country appears in so-called small press publications such as *Agni, The Kenyon Review, Field, Northwest Review,* and *Shenandoh.* The best among these small press publications receive thousands of submissions a month. *Writers Market* (Writer's Digest Books) does a good job of rating publications not only in terms of the likelihood of being published in them but also in terms of how they treat writers and their work. You would do well to consult this resource or others like it before sending off your work. Other excellent sources for small press publications include *International Directory of Little Magazines and*

Small Presses (Dustbooks) and *Directory of Literary Magazines* (The Council of Literary Magazines and Presses).

Writers Market also includes entries for commercial and trade publishers. If you are writing—or have written—a novel or saleable magazine article, check these categories in *Writers Market*.

Many publishers are reluctant to accept work directly from first-time novelists and deal only with literary agents. You might be best served by trying to obtain an agent, an accomplishment in its own right since agents make their living off successful books and do not spend their time on those projects that, in their view, do not have obvious commercial potential. There are many agent directories available, including *Writer's Guide to Book Editors, Publishers and Literary Agents* by Jeff Herman (Prima Publishing, Inc.). *Literary Agents: The Essential Guide for Writers* by Debby Mayer, published by Penguin USA in conjunction with Poets & Writers, Inc., is a very thorough, up-to-date directory that also contains several tips on finding and evaluating prospective agents. Also, if you know any publishing writers, you might ask them about their agents and perhaps get a reference.

With respect to magazines and journals, once you have identified a likely publication and familiarized yourself with its background, send for both a copy of the publication and its writer's guidelines. Find out as much as you can about the publication. Study the publication's guidelines to determine if your work fits stylistically, thematically, or otherwise. Most publications have their own vision and criteria for acceptable work, dictated as much by taste as by literary merit. For example, some publications do not accept "light" poetry or verse—or religious poetry or experimental fiction or essays about politics and so forth. Don't waste your time sending work to a publisher who will not even read it.

While it was rare in the past, these days several publications allow simultaneous submission of work to other publishers. If you do submit work to more than one publisher, be sure to notify each immediately if your work is published.

Contests and Vanity Presses

As with publishers in general, you would be well advised to research contests and vanity presses before submitting work to them—and particularly before paying any fees.

Vanity presses are publishers that writers pay to publish their work. Vanity presses that share publication and promotional costs with authors are sometimes called co-op presses. If you are interested only in seeing your work in print at any cost and regardless of whether anyone other than yourself sees it as worthwhile, then consider paying a vanity press to publish your writing. Such presses will also promote and advertise your work, for a fee. On the other hand, you might just consider producing a few volumes yourself using local printers.

Many contests charge entry fees ranging from $5 to $30, and these fees are often used to fund prizes, pay qualified judges, and otherwise administer the contests. Most of these contests are legitimate and use well-respected judges. However, beware of fly-by-night contests that promise publication or a handsome, bound volume of all winners (often, every submission is a winner) that may not use bona fide judges or panels of judges. New writers, like new musicians or other artists, often yearn for recognition and other ego satisfactions and are, therefore, vulnerable to illegal or quasilegal schemes intended to bilk them. Before you send in your submission or entry fee, see if you can find out who is sponsoring the contest—usually contests affiliated with colleges and universities are valid, as are those sponsored by literary or little magazines with long publication histories—and who the judges are—the best contests commission well-known writers to judge them.

Publishing on the Internet

The last few years have seen the emergence of a vast new venue for publication: the Internet. Hundreds of Web sites have sprung up that allow writers to share work with each other and with cyberspace in general. Writers with access to the Internet can submit their work to bulletin boards, ongoing forums, chat rooms, or on-line journals, some of which are offshoots of established paper publications, such as *Mississippi Review* (http://www.sushi.st.usm.edu/mrw), *The Missouri Review* (http://www.missouri.edu/~moreview), and others. As with hard-copy magazines and journals, most on-line publications maintain certain guidelines for submission, and you should go to the appropriate Web site to find them before submitting.

Unfortunately, copyright protections of work transmitted via Internet are hard to guarantee, but this is as true of the work of new writers as of established writers. Thousands of Web sites contain illegally obtained, copyright-protected material, and from time to time Web site authors are threatened with lawsuits if material is not removed. Since poetry, short fiction, and essays rarely involve significant monetary profit, the lack of copyright protection is seldom an issue, but you should be aware that when your work goes on the Internet, nothing prevents other people form using it.

HOW TO SUBMIT WORK

You can easily imagine how selective publishers can be if they are receiving thousands of submissions each month, which means that there is very little tolerance for work submitted that does not meet minimal standards of manuscript preparation. Again, study a publication's guidelines carefully, taking particular note of its instructions concerning manuscript mechanics. Of course, you should make every effort to insure that words are spelled correctly, that the grammar is correct, and that the manuscript is neat. Beyond this, most publications require that manuscripts abide by some or all of the requirements discussed in the following paragraphs.

Include a Very Brief Cover Letter

The cover letter should introduce you and your work succinctly and provide all relevant personal information, such as address and telephone number, as well as information about your writing and publishing background, including a list or bibliography of work you have published. However, bear in mind that this is not the place to "sell" your submission; the work should sell itself.

Groups of poems usually don't require a cover letter, unless there is a special reason to have one.

Include a Self-Addressed, Stamped Envelope

If you do *not* want the manuscript returned, which is increasingly the practice these days, but merely want a response, indicate this in your cover letter and include a self-addressed stamped envelope so that the publisher can send you an acceptance or rejection slip. If you do want your manuscript returned, be sure to include a self-addressed envelope and postage sufficient to accommodate your manuscript. (If you are sending work abroad, be sure to purchase the appropriate international coupons.)

Manuscript Mechanics

The following list of manuscript requirements is fairly standard; however, you should always obtain a copy of a publisher's submission guidelines. In the absence of guidelines, at least examine copies of the publication to which you are interested in submitting work.

- Use a good grade of paper, certainly not glossy FAX paper
- Double space
- Type or word process manuscripts
- Type only on one side of each page
- Leave at least one-inch margins all around
- Number the pages consecutively
- Include a title
- Include your last name at the top right-hand corner of every page

For Further Reading

Over the last twenty years, many books have been published that provide instruction in the various forms of creative writing, including fiction, poetry, and creative nonfiction. Some of these books include instruction in all forms of creative writing, while others focus on one kind or another. There are also many books on creative writing that seek mainly to inspire and motivate writers and would-be writers. Such books combine philosophy, wisdom, experience, mysticism, and psychology.

The following list of books includes only those that offer some instruction in the techniques or theories of creative writing. While several also include what might be considered inspirational material, their main emphasis is on technique. This is by no means an exhaustive list. Check your library or bookstore for more titles.

FICTION

Allen, Edward. *The Hands-On Fiction Workbook.* Upper Saddle River, NJ: Prentice Hall, 1996.

Bernays, Anne, and Pamela Painter. *What If?: Writing Exercises for Fiction Writers.* Revised and expanded edition. New York: HarperCollins, 1995.

Burroway, Janet. *Writing Fiction.* 4th ed. New York: Longman, 1996.

Cohen, Richard. *Writer's Mind: Crafting Fiction.* Lincolnwood (IL): NTC Publishing Group, 1995.

Gardner, John. *The Art of Fiction.* New York: Alfred A. Knopf, 1991.

Leebron, Fred, and Andrew Levy. *Creating Fiction: A Writer's Companion.* Fort Worth, TX: Harcourt Brace, 1995.

Willis, Meredith Sue. *Personal Fiction Writing.* New York: Teachers & Writers Collaborative, 1993.

POETRY

Rosenthal, M. L. *The Poet's Art.* New York: Norton, 1987.

Smith, Michael C. *Writing Dangerous Poetry.* Lincolnwood, IL: NTC/Contemporary Publishing, 1999.

The Teachers and Writers Handbook of Poetic Forms. Ed. Ron Padgett. New York: Teachers & Writers Collaborative, 1994.

Wallace, Robert. *Writing Poems.* 4th ed. New York: Longman, 1996.

CREATIVE NONFICTION

Gerard, Philip. *Creative Nonfiction*. Story Press Books, 1996.

Gutkind, Lee. *The Art of Creative Nonfiction: Writing and Selling the Literature of Reality*. John Wiley & Sons, 1997.

Zinsser, William. *On Writing Well*. 6th ed. New York: HarperCollins, 1998.

Zinsser, William. *Writing to Learn*. New York: HarperCollins, 1993.

MORE THAN ONE FORMAT

Bailey, Richard, et al. *The Creative Writer's Craft: Lessons in Poetry, Fiction, and Drama*. Lincolnwood, IL: NTC/Contemporary Publishing, 1999.

Bishop, Wendy. *Working Words: The Process of Creative Writing*. Mountain View, CA: Mayfield Publishing Company, 1992.

Burke, Carol, and Molly Best Tinsley. *The Creative Process*. New York: St. Martins, 1993.

DeMaria, Robert. *The College Handbook of Creative Writing*. 3rd ed. Fort Worth, TX: Harcourt Brace, 1998.

Kubis, Pat, and Bob Howland. *The Complete Guide to Writing Fiction and Nonfiction and Getting It Published*. Englewood Cliffs, NJ: Prentice Hall, 1990.

Mueller, Lavonne, and Jerry D. Reynolds. *Creative Writing: Forms and Techniques*. Lincolnwood (IL): NTC Publishing Group, 1992.

ORGANIZATIONS

The following organizations offer many good resources for creative writers, including newsletters, magazines, and books that provide information on conferences, contests, and getting published, as well as other resources for creative writing teachers and students. Again, this list is by no means exhaustive:

The Academy of American Poets, 548 Broadway, Suite 1208, New York, NY 10012-3250; Phone: (212) 274-0343; Fax: (212) 264-9427; Web site: http://www.poets.org

Associated Writing Programs, George Mason University, Tallwood House, Mail Stop 1E3, Fairfax, VA 22030; Phone: (703) 993-4301; Web site: http://web.gmu.edu/departments/awp

Poets and Writers, Inc., 72 Spring St., New York, NY 10012; Phone: (212) 226-3586; Web site: http://www.pw.org

Poetry Society of America, 15 Gramercy Park, New York, NY 10003; Phone: (212) 254-9628; Web site: http://www.bookwire.com/psa

Teachers and Writers Collaborative, 5 Union Square West, New York, NY 10003
Phone: (212) 691-6590

INTERNET RESOURCES AND PUBLICATIONS

Writers Club: http://www.writersclub.com

Writers Write: http://www.writerswrite.com

Poetry Daily: http://www.poems.com

World Wide Arts Resources: http://www.wwar.com

Acknowledgments

Banks, Russell. "The Neighbor" by Russell Banks appeared originally in *Esquire*. Reprinted by permission.

Beattie, Ann. Excerpt from *What Was Mine* by Ann Beattie. Reprinted by permission of Random House Inc. Excerpt from "The Longest Day of the Year" by Ann Beattie, from *What Was Mine*. Published by Random House. © 1991 by Irony and Pity, Inc.

Berryman, John. *#14* from *The Dream Songs* by John Berryman. Copyright © 1969 by John Berryman. Copyright renewed © 1997 by Kate Donahue Berryman. Reprinted by permission of Farrar, Straus & Giroux, Inc.

Bishop, Elizabeth. "One Art" from *The Complete Poems 1927–1979* by Elizabeth Bishop. Copyright © 1979, 1983 by Alice Helen Methfessel. Reprinted by permission of Farrar, Straus & Giroux, Inc.

Brooks, Colette. © 1988 by Colette Brooks from "Somewhere in the Eighties," an essay which appeared originally in *The Georgia Review,* Winter 1988. Reprinted by permission.

Buchwald, Art. From *Lighten Up, George* by Art Buchwald. Copyright © 1991 by Art Buchwald.

Carlson, Ron. From "Reading the Paper" by Ron Carlson, from *Sudden Fiction*. Reprinted by permission of the author.

Carver, Raymond. From *Cathedral* by Raymond Carver. Copyright © 1981, 1982, 1983 by Raymond Carver. Reprinted by permission of Alfred A. Knopf Inc. Excerpt from "Neighbors" by Raymond Carver, from *Where I'm Calling From*. Published by The Atlantic Monthly Press. Reprinted by permission of the publisher.

Coyle, Beverly. Excerpt from "The Baboon Hour" by Bevery Coyle from *The Kneeling Bus*. Copyright © 1990 by Beverly Coyle.

Didion, Joan. Excerpt from "The White Album" from *The White Album* by Joan Didion. Copyright © 1979 by Joan Didion. Reprinted by permission of Farrar, Straus & Giroux, Inc.

Grahn, Judy. "Ella in a Square Apron, along Highway 80" from *The Common Woman Poems* by Judy Grahn. © 1969 by Judy Grahn. Reprinted by permission of the author.

Kumin, Maxine. "How It Is," copyright © 1978 by Maxine Kumin, from *Selected Poems 1960–1990* by Maxine Kumin. Reprinted by permission of W. W. Norton & Company, Inc.

Lux, Thomas. "How to Cure Your Fever" by Thomas Lux. Appeared originally in *Emerson Review*. Reprinted by permission of the author.

Martin, Lee. "The Least You Need to Know" from *The Least You Need to Know* by Lee Martin. Copyright © 1996 by Lee Martin. Reprinted by permission of Sarabande Books.

Morris, John. Reprinted with the permission of Scribner, a Division of Simon & Schuster Inc., from *The Life Beside This One* by John N. Morris. Copyright © 1975 John N. Morris.

Neruda, Pablo. An excerpt from the poem "Ode to My Socks" by Pablo Neruda from *Neruda and Valejo: Selected Poems*, edited and translated by Robert Bly. Published by Beacon Press. Copyright © 1967, 1976 by Robert Bly, reprinted with his permission.

O'Brien, Tim. "The Things They Carried" from *The Things They Carried*. Copyright © 1990 by Tim O'Brien. Reprinted by permission of Houghton Mifflin Co./Seymour Lawrence. All rights reserved.

O'Connor, Flannery. Excerpt from "A Good Man is Hard to Find" *in A Good Man Is Hard to Find and Other Stories*, copyright 1953 by Flannery O'Connor and renewed 1981 by Regina O'Connor, reprinted by permission of Harcourt, Inc. Excerpt from "Everything That Rises Must Converge" from *Everything That Rises Must Converge* by Flannery O'Connor. Copyright © 1962, 1965 by the Estate of Mary Flannery O'Connor and copyright renewed © 1993 by Regina O'Connor. Reprinted by permission of Farrar, Straus & Giroux, Inc.

O'Connor, Frank. From *Collected Stories* by Frank O'Connor. Copyright 1951 by Frank O'Connor. Reprinted by permission of Alfred A. Knopf Inc.

O'Hara, Frank. Excerpt from "Steps" by Frank O'Hara. © 1964 by Frank O'Hara. Reprinted by permission of City Lights Books.

Ordan, David. From "Any Minute Mom Should Come Blasting Through the Door" by David Ordan, originally published in *TriQuarterly 62* (Winter 1985). Reprinted by permission.

Plumly, Stanley. "Brothers and Sisters" by Stanley Plumly, from *Out-of-the-Body-Travel*. Reprinted by permission of the author.

Subject Index

incorporating, 42
originality through, 180–81
Development, recording, 2–7
Dialog
    characterization through, 156–59
    in essays, 195
    and hidden emotions, 55, 143–45
    tag lines, 157
Dictionary, computer, 16–17
Dinner table, 41–44
Discomfort, working beyond, 17–18
Documents, personal, 45–47
Doubletalk, 143–45

E

Editing
    beginnings, 197
    facts, 182
    flashbacks, 193
    overwriting and, 180
    poetry, 192
Electronic publishing, 202
Elements, the, 126–28
Emotions
    author's, 17–18
    clichéd, 182, 184
    clues to, 139
    and dialog, 156–59
    hidden, 55, 68, 143–45
    honest, 182
    incorporating, 38
    motivations, 81–82, 179
Engaging an expression, 134
Environment
    setting, 146–48, 194
    as source of ideas, 198
Essays
    criteria for, 22–23, 127
    and unblocking, 195–96
Evaluating your work, 176–86
    characters, 179
    clichés, 183–85
    critiques, 177
    emotional honesty, 182
    humor, 185
    involvement, 177–79
    logbook and, 2–7
    originality, 180–81

premature criticism, 17–18
tension, 182–83
Excuses, exploring, 81–83
Exercises, recording, 2–7
External conflict, 182

F

Facts, editing, 182
Feelings. *See* emotions
Fiction writing
    criteria for, 21–22, 127
    unblocking, 193–95
Figurative language. *See* imagery; metaphors
Finish, determining, 190
Flashbacks, 193
Flaws, exploring, 118–20
Focused freewriting, 8–9
Form, choosing, 20–23, 127
Frauds, contest, 202
Free association, 11–13, 71
Freewriting, 8–9
Freshness. *See* originality
Freudian slip, 11, 82
Friendship, exploring, 96–98
Furniture, 34–36

G

Games as creative helps, 13
Getting lost, exploring, 78–80
Gossip, exploring, 108–11
Guidelines, publisher's, 201

H

Hidden emotions. *See* emotions
History, personal, 45–47, 63–66
Home contractors, 51–53
Honesty, emotional, 182
Humanity of characters, 179
Humor, evaluating, 185

I

Ideas. *See* creativity
Imagery
    and characterization, 149–51
    clichéd, 132
    and poetry, 20–21
    and relationships, 164–66
    See also metaphors

Author/Title Index